EVOLUTION OF A PSYCHIATRIST

EVOLUTION OF A PSYCHIATRIST
Against the Odds

Kenneth J Headen, MD

ISBN : 1-59457-522-3

To order additional copies, please contact us.
BookSurge, LLC
www.booksurge.com
1-866-308-6235
orders@booksurge.com

EVOLUTION OF A PSYCHIATRIST

TABLE OF CONTENTS

INTRODUCTION

They said I couldn't be a doctor. I must be still dreaming. Now they say I can't write a book. I have never paid *They* any attention. Had I done that, this book would not exist. You, the readers, are probably wondering "*Who does this guy think he is? What makes him feel so important that someone would want to spend precious time reading his autobiography? I could understand if he were of the stature of a Colin Powell, a Denzel Washington, or a Michael Jordan. And what could he write about his dull and boring life that would be of any value to anyone?*" If you've come this far, it didn't happen by accident. There really is a reason for everything that happens.

The lives of the rich and famous are no more important than the lives of ordinary people making up our world. We all have an interesting story to tell, when it's presented correctly. Celebrities are important only because we *choose* to believe that they are. The human spirit and psyche have always yearned for objects to admire. The media of television, radio, and written prose are man-made creations that allow us to project the *image* of godlike power, through those chosen for exposure, to the ***attention of many at once.*** Like a magic trick, masses of people are hypnotized into placing much more value upon certain individuals than they place on themselves. Giving it no thought, people assume that those chosen few are automatically more intelligent, more loving, and live more interesting and important lives than those of us not exposed to such attention. That belief, in itself, is a delusion of grandeur shared by the celebrated. The whole world is insane; by the same token, the creativity of the human mind assures that life will never become boring. We convince ourselves that we know these celebrities as we would a close family member. If you met that person in reality, the delusion could be damaged or totally destroyed. At that moment, you would realize that the whole reality had been created in your mind. Those in powerful positions are betting all they have that awakening from these delusions will never happen. They understand the public's need for idols, as well as its need for a dose of magic and a sedative to distract its collective consciousness from less pleasing thoughts.

The ultimate truth is that celebrities aren't a bit more important or more blessed than you and I. The power they possess is given directly to them by those who expose their image to many at once and, indirectly, by the public at large, that chooses to share the delusion in order to fulfill our psychological need for icons of good or evil. Concisely, the concept of celebrity is essentially a projected, grandiose delusion that one can choose to accept or to see it for what it really is. Most choose to accept the delusion as fact, and when the current celebrity's magic begins to fade or the sedative starts to wear down, that image is replaced by a fresh one, created to perpetually feed this constant craving. Understanding the psychology of the public toward the media is what gives me the audacity to write this book. Due to my lack of exposure to those capable of giving my work exposure to many at once, this book may only be read by a limited number of people. Knowing this didn't stop me from writing it. Those who appreciate authenticity and originality will find their way to the book. They will understand that quality and value have nothing to do with marketing methodology and media control by certain executives, but that the real power exists with us ordinary people. We just choose to believe and share the delusion sold to the public and perpetuated by those mainly interested in lining their pockets with your money. I am not the least bit motivated by money, but by a desire to put some of my memories and ideas on paper. I think my life has been extremely interesting, dramatic, and at times hilarious. At this point in my life I have the desire to share some of the highlights of my life with those who might be interested. I strongly encourage others to create their own written history of their time spent on the planet, so that *They* will get the story right when you have passed away. You might be amazed at who finds it to be of value.

To the lay public in general, the role of the clinical psychiatrist is often misunderstood. Unlike most medical specialties, patients can be involuntarily thrust into treatment if considered a threat to self or others. Many patients harbor underlying contempt for the very person from whom they seek help, often resulting in game playing and self-defeating behaviors. In order to provide optimal psychiatric treatment, the doctor must be capable of unusual objectivity. This requires integration of many different skills. The first challenge involves engaging the patient to extract information, which may depend solely on the motivation, ability, and intent of the patient. The subjective information shared by the patient enhances the doctors' ability to perform an accurate mental status examination, which is a mental snapshot of the examinee that includes mental and written documentation. This exam must be performed with or without cooperation from a patient, someone who may have no concept that the process is occurring. In a relatively short period of time, data must be collected about the patient's appearance, movement, speech, attitude, mood and affect; thought content of suicidal or homicidal ideation; perceptual abnormalities such as hallucinations, delusions, or paranoia; cognitive abilities including orientation to person, place, and time; abstracting ability; immediate, short- and long-term memory; simple calculations; general intellect; fund of knowledge; and, finally, data about the level of judgment ability and patient's insight level into their own condition. This probably seems to be too much information to collect in a few minutes. The fascinating thing is that this is only a piece of the diagnostic formula which may also require a comprehensive lab work-up, including blood chemistries, hematology, toxic screens, endocrine function, vitamin b12, folic acid, testing for latent syphilis or newly acquired HIV infection. A thorough work-up may also include C.A.T. scans, M.R.I., E.K.G., E.E.G., or other medical testing. Further work-up may include psychological testing for personality traits, mood or psychotic disorder, developmental disorder, learning disorder, or intellectual abilities. If more information is required to aid diagnosis or treatment, the work-up continues even further. All of the above-mentioned data is formulated to present a reasonable diagnosis, which requires a decision of which treatment to choose. Treatment will consist of medications, group and individual therapies, safety precautions, and monitoring the effect of this treatment.

Often, after such an extensive work-up, the psychiatrist has to deal with the patient's ability to comply with treatment. It is not uncommon to hear a number of excuses, such as *I don't like taking pills* or *Only those blue pills work for me.* We also hear *I'm allergic to all medications except Xanax* and *That medicine makes me feel funny* or *I didn't know I was suppose to take that one too.* The media has contributed to this behavior with information that is biased at best, and rarely supplied within the proper context or perspective. Such information, when not properly interpreted can lead to mass hysteria. Other stressors for the practitioner include unnecessary bother with managed care organizations, being told which medications can and cannot be used (a decision totally based upon the price of the medication, not on what's the best medication for the patient). More time is wasted appealing cases for reimbursement. There are times that payment is denied for the most trivial of billing errors, such as using the wrong billing code. Each year, many thousands of dollars are never collected. Sometimes precious time is wasted on the phone as we bargain with these companies to get one more day of treatment for the patient. The 50% total tax burden and overhead expense are also facts of life, in the ever-changing world of private practice. Additionally, there is the ever-present burden of the doctor having to comply with hospital policies and deadlines. Finally, there is the family of the patient, who may themselves be struggling with feelings of guilt and fear, or with an untreated mental illness. Family members have the potential to greatly enhance or hamper the outcome of a patient's treatment. Many psychiatrists are opting to leave the profession altogether, figuring it's no longer worth the hassle. The process of mental health reform will not be considered for discussion here, due to its cryptic nature. Also, at this time, there's no reliable means of estimating the final outcome.

A multidisciplinary team approach from several mental health specialists—this includes nursing, social workers, psychologists, therapists, C.N.A.'s, technicians, ward clerks, students, and others—is required to carry out the whole inpatient process. A totally new team will be required for certain patients, when outpatient and maintenance treatment begin. A good psychiatrist has to be a team player. He or she is the Captain of an all-star Treatment Team, assembled to stamp out pestilence and disease. Actually, the more realistic goal of the treatment team is to attempt to provide whatever is necessary to help the patient return to the community and live as independently and happily as possible. This however, is much easier said than done.

Psychiatric medicine is on the cutting edge, from pharmaceutical agents for treating minor ailments from insomnia to severe mental conditions, the type that may have been a long sentence into a mental institution sixty or seventy years ago. We're talking about illnesses such as schizoaffective disorder, schizophrenia, severe personality disorders, aggressive behavioral disorders, or severe cases of bipolar mood disorder *(manic-depressive illness)*. With the newer medications available, it is now possible for a low functioning patient to have a much-improved quality of life. Psychoanalysis or extensive insight-oriented psychotherapy are impractical to use for the vast majority of patients. It simply isn't affordable for most, and certainly not cost-effective for managed care organizations. Such treatments, though commonly fantasized by the general public as being the epitome of a psychiatrists' work, are actually considered a luxury and available only to a small portion of the public. Technological advances hold the most promise for effectively treating illnesses, which previously we were unable to successfully treat. In our lifetime, we could witness cures or prevention for conditions such as Alzheimer's dementia, Parkinson's disease, certain cancers, and even AIDS. These advances will inevitably be achieved in much the same way as conditions from the past, such as organ transplants and artificial joints and limbs, and the eradication of public health plagues like polio, small pox, and syphilis. At one point, these accomplishments were considered out of reach. We will be challenged, however, to not have our technology get too far ahead of our ethics, which is already a problem with issues such as when it is reasonable to cease treating patients and allow them a death with dignity, as opposed to becoming brain dead and having to be unplugged from a respirator. For all involved, that can be even more traumatic than allowing a natural death. Who is to play the role of God here?

As an intern, I was involved with treating a young woman who had battled renal failure. She was also afflicted with other medical and mental conditions that made her life very unpleasant. This patient and her family chose to let Nature take its course, instead of putting her through daily dialysis, having her undergo kidney transplants, and facing a continued poor quality of life. As a modern-thinking physician, it really affected me to see a lucid, alert, and talking patient gradually become lethargic, drift into a coma, and eventually die, as family members waited at her bedside. It was so hard to stand idly by and administer nothing more than a sip of water. Most doctors are trained to preserve life at all reasonable costs. This situation was so against that manner of thought. However, there did seem to be a certain peace about allowing things to occur naturally. She had the opportunity to say good-bye to her family and to pass away in her sleep. As is often the case, she waited until everyone left the room for a break, early the next morning, before taking her last breath. All through that night, instead of heroic measures to keep the patient alive, my role was to comfort the family and try to make her death as comfortable as possible. The encounter had become an emotional and spiritual experience, rather than the panic and chaos one usually expects to see in a modern hospital.

I never had a clue about what I would do when growing up and leaving home for college, but my calling was always to be a psychiatrist. I now know that I could never be totally content or happy in any other medical specialty—or any other job, for that matter. This particular type of work is what I was born to do. It is why I endured the hardships, why I often pushed ahead in the darkness to reach my goal, even when my focus became dim and I had thoughts of walking away from the path. God was always there with me; I just forgot how to communicate with the Creator. There were times when I was sure God had left me, but eventually I discovered that He had never been gone, not even for one second. It was I who had been gone.

People sometimes say that to be a psychiatrist you are probably *crazy* yourself and are most likely trying to solve your own issues. The truth of the matter is that deep down, we psychiatrists are just as human as everyone else. We seek the exact same things from life as everyone else, but we are capable of doing it at a more insightful level. We understand the physical realm *(the body)* as well as any humans who ever walked the planet. We probably know the function of the mind better than most, too. These two beliefs entail two-thirds of the essence of a whole human being. I choose to go all the way and attempt to master the spiritual aspect as well. I believe it will become clear during the course of this book that I have faced the exact same problems most others have faced in their lives.

Crazy is a lay person's term, meaning a relative state that visits us all from time to time. It is usually not the person who is crazy, but the situation in which people find themselves. Some people seem to prefer craziness; if they choose to spend their lives leaving one craziness for another, more power to them. Craziness is not against the law, until people are at risk of harm because of it. Sometimes, craziness is the only thing that keeps one sane. That's because reality can become too difficult to face and to endure. Craziness can sometimes be a coping mechanism. I always tell my patients that they are not the insanity, but that the insanity lies within their situation and circumstances. How does a sane individual adapt to insane circumstances? Medicines will set the stage and give one the stamina to battle back, but stress comes with but one purpose: to destroy you. Stress diminishes the body's ability to fight invasion from microorganisms and cancer cells; stress raises the blood pressure, which damages the organs; and stress imbalances the healthy chemical balance of the body, thereby setting the stage for diseases to occur. Stress will not cease until you are lying in your casket. That is, unless you develop a way to change your situation or change yourself, so that the stress loses effect. This can only be truly accomplished by tapping into the limitless power of the mind, in addition to the rediscovery of the union with one's spirit and soul. The key word here is change. Change absolutely must occur. There can be only one result when a sane individual is somehow in the midst of an abnormal or detrimental situation and they refuse to do what is necessary for change to occur. That person experiences maladaptation. The mind and body flood them with clues to get the hell out of there, but they often interpret the clues as an illness. Feeling helpless, soon the mind develops a real *illness (separation from sanity and from God)*. This is the state the person is usually in when they arrive for treatment. That is, if they are fortunate enough to make it to treatment.

One of the things I like most about being a psychiatrist is the holistic approach undertaken with the appropriate patient. Holistic means mind, body, and soul, and not just seeing the disease, but also seeing the whole person. In my view, we were created as triune beings. Therefore, when one part is ill, the other two parts usually won't go unaffected. A person without some spiritual connection will have a hard time remaining sane through this often unpredictable human life. If one believes that this earth is *all there is,* and becomes too attached to it, that person is destined for unhappiness. I believe that in ultimate reality, this earth is a temporary stage for the dramas of our lives, but one day the curtain inevitably must close. Everything in the physical world changes and eventually passes away. Our true home is in the spiritual realm. Even a brain and a mind will one day grow dim and pass away, but the soul endures forever.

If you are one who does not take life too seriously, you will enjoy this book. I hope that it will inspire some to believe they can successfully pursue their calling, if the willingness to endure is there. For others I hope it will demonstrate the absurdness of petty behaviors, such as intolerance of those who have different physical characteristics or cultures. I hope that one day those intolerant people will finally realize that we are all in this together. We all are brothers and sisters who I believe are the progeny of the *exact* same two grand ancestors, the least common denominators of mankind. This is the core principal for which Dr. King died prematurely. Logic dictates that there exist countless common denominators tracing the path from God to the origin of time through the present. Scientific theory suggests that the entire universe began from an infinitely small point. If a mind can conceive this, it can just as likely conceive that the concept of *impossible* is just a creation of our minds, suggesting that human reality is just one of infinite realities. I find this to be as plausible as the book of Genesis' account of the Garden of Eden with its serpent personification of Satan. It therefore is self evident that either belief system supports the *possibility* of anything the mind can comprehend.

Evolution is not an evil or apocryphal word, as some have been frightened into believing. It actually has little or nothing to do with apes turning into humans. Even Creationists must acknowledge the real existence of an evolutionary process that occurs all around us all the time. The idea of evolution is frightening and instantly rejected by one with a closed mind, or is intellectually challenged, or has intense fear of death. Often these are the people for whom many religions were designed, and there is absolutely nothing wrong with that. Certain religions once denounced the existence of dinosaurs even with clear existence of fossil records. The only logic given for this belief is the lack of Biblical documentation. Psychiatry eventually rescinded the legitimacy of homosexuality as a mental illness due to insufficient scientific evidence. In most fundamentalist religious doctrine, homosexuals will eternally be an abomination punishable by eternal fire and brimstone.

Slavery would not have been viable without support from the church, neither would the belief that the world was flat, going as far as punishing Galileo harshly for thinking otherwise. God never said the world was flat, man did. Man is *not* infallible. I believe that God is not anally retentive and eternally rigid or neurotically fixated on eternal damnation of his own creations. Pardon my saying so, but maybe God can even change his mind once and a while, with mans permission of course. I firmly believe that all things are revealed in time if we are ready to receive. Even our knowledge evolves, if we allow it the opportunity to do so. The entire universe is in a constant state of evolution, and believe it or not, God created it this way. If not, then who did? In appearance, humans evolved differently simply because of a need to adapt to different climates and conditions in the geographical locations to which humans migrated from the cradle of civilization. Concisely, the vehicle housing our souls, known as our body is a dynamically miraculous but transient multi-system configuration of trillions of synchronized living cells, biochemicals, trace metals, and minerals, held together in a water base and existing in the four known of countless dimensions in which God has arranged reality. God designed diversity as a test of our ability to love. When you hate your brother, ultimately, you hate yourself, and you will be the one who loses precious time and energy for an insane activity. You will be the one who loses when all is said and done.

To my mother Ruth for having me, my sister Alfreda for showing me the path, Betty Alexander for believing in me, my friend Lawrence for keeping me laughing, and my wife Pia for standing by me.

CHAPTER 1

Early Imprinting

Is This it? No More Cards?

It all began one cold Sunday evening, December 14, 1958. A new soul entered this planet we call earth. Greenish, light brown eyes opened and peered around the delivery room. I imagine the doctor thinking to himself, "Colored babies with this appearance are pretty rare. I wonder who his daddy is." This is a question to which the newborn would one day seek an answer. Nevertheless, at this point it remained a mystery for most. The newborn arrived at his new home, where there was a nice fire burning and two teenage girls keeping their 70-year-old grandmother company. *"Ruth's got the baby, let me see him, don't drop him, I need to sit down and rest, where is Larry? He talked about wanting to see his new baby brother so badly, he went down to Margie and Johnny's looking for Lewis, bring him here Afreda, Phyllis, one of you. He's a pretty baby,"* These words modestly simulate the spirit of that morning. Later that day, there was chatter about what to name the baby. *"I don't know. If it had been a girl, I had a name for her,"* stated Ruth. Somebody broke the following silence with, *"Let's name him Kenneth, Kenneth J. What does J stand for? Jay, just like it sounds. Kenneth, Ken Jay Lineberry."* And so Ken became the new member of the family and was the center of attention for days to come.

The Lineberry family was (is) a pretty colorful cast of characters. Not too affectionate but just as loving as most. Ruth had become pregnant as a teenager, and after a 12-year break she started to trust men a little more. She had become hardened with disdain for most men, since she had known heartbreak and disappointment from her last three relationships. She was sure Otis would not be so irresponsible and abandon her. Otis was good looking and so nice. And so *married* for his second time. Ruth had no idea until it was too late. Despite that, she developed an attitude of "I'll do it my damn self. I'm through with men forever. People can think what they want to. I know my child won't be like all the other men." And so Ruth continued her role as single mother, a role she had become accustomed to over the past eighteen years. Sooner or later, most of the extended family accepted that this was the way things were going to be, and it became taboo to discuss such issues among the family. At least, that is, where it could be heard.

The house was old and small for the number of people raised there. It had around five rooms, with a front porch, plus a back porch facing an old unpainted barn. When it rained, I loved the sound of raindrops hitting its tin roof.

There was no such thing as a shower. For the first few years of my life, we collected all the water we needed from an old spring and filled buckets or one of those large metal tubs. During weekdays, a quick wash in the foot tub or basin was sufficient. But on Saturday nights, I remember fitting just fine in that metal tub and getting a good wash in preparation for Sunday School and church at Gee's Grove. Other business, the more personal kind, was handled in the outhouse that was situated up the hill from the house.

I think Julius Clarence and Ma'Berta Siler Lineberry had about twelve children, most of them boys, and most with that fatal alcohol gene that resulted in the loss of much potential. In retrospect, I have a hunch there was a strong gene for bipolar mood disorder as well. The only option for dealing with those unpredictable mood shifts and inappropriate behaviors was to take a little drink, followed by another drink. There clearly were some paranoid behaviors in ancestors such as Great Grandpa Newton Lineberry, who had moved to Chatham County from some northerly place. He was a Caucasian who openly loved black women. I suspect he was a little paranoid: he sprinkled flour all around the house before leaving, just so he could detect an intruder's footprints. Grandpa Newton died young, and of suspicious causes. He was last seen alive hanging out with white boys at the local swimming hole. This was rarely discussed in my nuclear family, but Ma'Berta held that story, and many other fascinating ones, in her mind.

Julius also died relatively young, of cardiovascular disease. Had he been alive to benefit from today's medical knowledge, his life might have been extended by many more years.

All of the children were grown and dispersed here and there, and some there and here again. Ruth had spent time in the New York area, but was settled down and resigned to taking care of *Mama*, since she was advancing in age. It was a job that she sometimes detested, evident in the piercing stares she'd give Mama when she would start to get on Ruth's nerves. Mama received a meager social security check, which she safeguarded in her brazier during the daytime and under her mattress at night. She would help out with the groceries and the light bill.

Ruth (*as I referred to my mother*) was known to be a hard and dependable worker. She eventually settled for a job at Brewer's Laundry, a privately run business in Siler City. To my knowledge, we never asked for a welfare check, even though we lived much below the poverty line. I suppose it was pride, but I never knew we were poor until I was older and able to compare. I think that is when my psychological issues began. But we seemed to do well, only having to depend on others for transportation. I eventually grew to hate this dependency.

One advantage to living with Mama was that some of her children and relatives were always willing to help in any way they could. And the village did help raise the child during that time. That basically meant there was no immunity from a good butt whipping, no matter where you were. Remember that this was before indoor plumbing and only a few people had a telephone. However, I do remember almost everyone having a television set.

Johnny Foxx was the greatest man I new during those early years. Johnny was married to Margie, Ruth's sister, and they lived next door. Margie was blessed with a brilliant sense of humor, making her often fun to be around. Johnny often referred to me as Kennus. I couldn't wait to get up in the morning and see what Johnny had planned. He owned a tractor, which he used for plowing everyone's garden. He would let me sit in his lap and sometimes steer, which I loved. When I was a little older, I'd walk behind the plow and collect worms for fishing bait. Sometimes I think Johnny's daughter, Jeanette, was envious of the attention he gave me, but she was in school and away most of the day. Lewis, the older child was entering manhood and rarely involved with everyday domestic concerns. Some days I found Johnny lying on the couch, sick on the stomach to the point of vomiting. I felt bad when Johnny was sick. I was probably an adult before realizing that he was having bad hangovers, from too much alcohol. The only thing I knew about alcohol was that it was a very bad thing. Johnny had lost his right arm in a sawing accident several years before, but he was able to do more with one arm than most men could manage with two. It didn't bother me that Johnny only had one arm. In fact, I thought it was cool and sometimes pretended that I only had one arm. Johnny had all kinds of trucks, tools, and gadgets, so it was always exciting to see what Johnny had planned. Would we haul firewood on the pickup? Would we carry slabs on the larger truck? Or maybe we'd ride up to the Country Store for Cracker Jacks, the kind with a prize in the box.

Johnny built a trailer to hook up to my tricycle. I was so proud of that trailer and I would drive around hauling wood, just like Johnny. One day, as I was playing in the dirt, a rooster jumped on my back and started pecking my neck. I was terrified and began to yell. Johnny ran out of the house, picked up a chain, and threw it at the rooster, running him away. After knowing that I was all right, he and Margie had a good laugh about what that rooster was trying to do to me. I did not think it was very funny. From that day forward, I had rooster phobia

I now understand that Margie and Johnny were probably

tired of seeing me every day, but I never got that feeling, However, I would cry whenever they left together, or as a family, and I wasn't able to go. I found myself crying often, so I guess I needed a lot of love and a lot of attention. I had a hard time learning that I did not have to be the center of attention all the time, that I didn't have to pitch the softball during family games, and that I didn't have to be the one to hide the Easter eggs.

My brother, Larry, hated crybabies and I remember him angrily telling me to stop that crying. I needed more than that. I now see that the important thing was to have an adult understand my reason for crying, and deal with it from that perspective.

As I got older, I was spending most of my time around women. Johnny couldn't be there as much and I cried when I couldn't go to the hairdresser with my sisters and Ruth and they would run me back to the house. I vividly remember one day when I obsessively demanded that my mother wave goodbye to me from the van that stopped along the highway to pick her up for work. She got in and I started waving out the living room window. She didn't appear to wave back so I started crying and I told myself that I was really going to let her have it that evening. She had left me a quarter, which was big money to me in 1964. I accidentally dropped it in a crack where the window sill should have been. I tried and tried, but I could not retrieve it. It was not a good day.

My Uncle Cola, left mentally challenged from childhood febrile seizures, taught me to count the cars on the freight train that passed by every morning. That became a morning ritual. Though his IQ was probably 65, and there was usually an odor of white liquor and onions on his breath, Uncle Cola was my first math teacher, demonstrating there being no need to be of genius stature to learn arithmetic. Family members have told me of the day I came close to being killed by a car while running across the busy highway to greet Uncle Cola. There must have been a guardian angel watching over me. Eventually, I began to dislike my uncle for many years because of his alcoholism and

tendency to come in the house and curse out Mama and Ruth.
Were I a bit older, I'm sure that would have not continued. As
you read along a bit further, it will become clearer what I mean
by that statement. Uncle Cola was actually almost adorable
when he wasn't drinking, even quite affectionate on occasion.
"Come here Kenna and give your uncle a hug, I'm gonna give
you something one day." The worst part about that was rubbing
against that abrasive beard. Once, while sitting quietly on the
old trunk in the den, he kicked me in the chin for picking and
annoying him. Retrospectively, I know it was mostly a reflex
response and I probably deserved it, because I could be quite
a nuisance at times. He was reprimanded by his brother for the
act, so I suppose it was better I learn that lesson of self control
from him, than from a less caring stranger.

One day, a big rainstorm came. When it had nearly ceased,
we went out on the back porch and sat down. My mother saw a
long black object in the garden beside the barn. *"Ken, go see what
that is."* Being the obedient son, I walked down the slope toward
the unidentified object. As I approached it, it started to move
and then it dawned on me that this was the biggest, blackest
snake known to man. I panicked and began screaming at the top
of my lungs, "SNAKE! SNAKE! Ruth, it's a snake! I supposed
that the snake had come from under the barn, for a little drink
and to cool off. During that time, the word *snake* in rural black
culture was a Code Red alert. Whether the snake was black,
brown, green, poisonous or non-poisonous, you absolutely had
to kill it. Ruth yelled to me, "There's Johnny leaving in the car,
tell him to come and shoot it!" Things seemed to be happening
in slow motion. "Johnny! Johnny!! Snake! Snake!!" Johnny
couldn't hear me and he drove away in the midst of my desperate
pleas. The snake was so big that it seemed to be barely able to
move. I still remember that feeling of helplessness. The snake
was crawling back under the barn, Johnny was driving away, and
I did not know what to do. Ruth, and maybe Phyllis, came to
make sure the snake returned under the barn. It was never to be
seen again. A similar scene would occur at least once more, but
with a king snake crawling under a plank bridge. I had recurring

dreams about snakes for years. Why are black people so afraid
of snakes? I believe it is because if you were bitten in the olden
days, you were probably doomed to suffer, and maybe even die.
Simply put, that was your ass.

One of my final early childhood terrors occurred with
Ruth and Phyllis, while walking down the railroad to visit
neighbors. Walking on the railroad was very common and there
were always stories about some unfortunate soul who fell asleep
on the tracks, probably drunk, and ended up losing a leg—or
worse. This particular evening, the freight train decided to pay
us a visit. This was not unlike the snake scene, except that I
started yelling "Train!" and Ruth screamed, "Catch him Phyllis!"
which fortunately she did. We were able to move to safety as
the train passed. I have no doubt that there has always been
a Guardian Angel with me, keeping me alive for some reason.
When I reminisce about the dozens of times I could have been
killed, it confirms to me that God has other plans.

One day, Johnny's son, Lewis, came home with a wife and
three children: Gary, Annette, and Priscilla. I ran and jumped
on my tricycle (with the wagon towed behind), trying to show
off. Of course, everyone wanted to ride and I don't think I got it
back that day. That's when I realized I was going to have to learn
to share, and this became even more certain when Lewis's new
mobile home arrived. Our house would now be in the middle,
next to our new neighbors and my new playmates. Johnny and I
were never as close again

CHAPTER 2

The Monster Within

Please Don't Feed the Monster

Ruth, who is my daddy?" With a somewhat troubled look, she said, "Your daddy is Otis, Otis Headen." Where is he, why doesn't he live with us? How come he's my daddy, did he ask to be my daddy? "You'll understand when you get older." Is he Alfreda, Phyllis, and Larry's daddy, too?" A little irritated, she would say "No! Now stop asking so many questions." Eventually I stopped and I now understand. It remained a taboo subject and I felt badly for my siblings, sometimes just being known as Ruth's boy or Ruth's girls and having no involvement from a father while growing up. Something was not fair about that. In reality, it has not been a factor. What's more, it's true that a child is much better off without a father, than having a bad one, especially considering all the negative Karma that can produce. In the ultimate truth, I now know that how you get here does not matter one iota in the eyes of God. It's all about the kind of person you are, the kind of life you lead through the choices you make. Any judgment from any human being is insignificant and reveals not only the degree of ignorance, but also the personality flaws of one who judges.

One day in 1964, while I was on the floor playing with my trains and trucks and watching Lucy or Andy Griffith with my grandmother, who kept me during the daytime, there was a knock at the door. Two men appeared and asked Mama to take me with them for a ride. As we rode, one of them told me he was my daddy. We went uptown and he bought me some blowing bubbles and a ball and glove. I felt pretty good when I returned, but I was too young to have an interest in baseball. That ball and glove sat in the corner until, one day, it was removed by one of my cousins, never to be returned again. My daddy took me to town, and that was just wonderful. I'm so glad that I have a daddy. I was discouraged from telling people who my daddy was and I couldn't use his name on any forms for school the following year. In fact, Ruth or Phyllis erased it from the paper after I had written it in. What the hell was going on here? It didn't make any sense. I was visited by my dad every now and then, but I was made to feel that I shouldn't be proud about it. Do I or don't I have a daddy? This was my greatest childhood issue and it caused me considerable conflict. Usually, if a nosey schoolmate persistently asked who my daddy was, I'd go mute and start to cry. Why was so much importance placed on who my father was? Since I didn't have a father at home, I began to think this was a terrible thing and that maybe I was inferior to other people.

Before starting school, I engaged in some behaviors that I feel badly about even today. I can only hope that God has forgiven me. I was not always the smart little good boy, as I presented myself. Sometimes I would act out plays in the cold living room, while Mama was in the room that had the fire. Roy Rodgers was my hero and Dale Evans was my girlfriend. I got this funny feeling in my loins when I thought of her. What the heck is going on there? Anyway, we always caught the bad guys. I would take my sisters' record collection and play Frisbee with them, destroying many, I'm sure. And I should never have gotten together with any of my cousins, J.C.'s kids. We became instant weapons of mass destruction for anything we came across. Maybe it was therapeutic for us to bash the windows out of old cars for no reason, or to knock each other in the head with dirt balls and throw rocks at passing cars. On the other hand, maybe we were just poorly supervised and ignorant as hell. Anyway, the thing I regret the most, and which I now realize borders on delinquency, was killing some or most of a litter of puppies from the barn. I wasn't violent with them, but my stupid ass kept throwing them in the little stream (or the *branch*, as we called it) just to see them swim out. I don't remember exactly, but I do know that some of them died, if not all. I think I had been watching too many cartoons on TV and I hadn't developed a concept of death. I never saw Huckleberry Hound or Yogi Bear die. They could live through anything. I'm glad today's TV wasn't around then. Of course, now I wish that the mother dog would have caught me and bit a plug from my rump. At least then I wouldn't still be feeling so guilty about it. It would have been worth it, getting bitten or chased away.

I've had my share of bullies all my life. Interestingly, most of them died young. I don't know why, but I truly believe that God has watched over me. And that's even throughout the moronic parts of my life, of which there have been many episodes. One of my neighbors was a few years older and was very mischievous. Even though he preaches the gospel of Jesus Christ today, he taught me every curse word I knew and...and even helped me pronounce them correctly. My Aunt Margie and I visited him and his mother one day. He and I went into his room, where he had an abundance of toys that I hoped to play with. Instead, he wanted to show me how to fight, illustration included. I knew nothing about fighting. He beat the shit out of me, throwing me against a chair and causing my brow to bleed profusely. He told me not to tell anyone, which I never did. He got a Band-aid from the cabinet and fixed the wound. I still have the scar. Another time, I went to visit kinfolk with my grandmother. Dennis, who is now deceased, was there to be my playmate for the day. He was bigger and older than I and he threw me, kicked me, tripped me, and verbally abused me, while the adults had an afternoon of leisurely conversation. I began to realize that Dennis wasn't wrapped too tight, but I'd never been exposed to violence, nor had I been shown how to defend myself. I went to my grandmother for help, but she told me to go outdoors and play with Dennis. So Dennis kicked my ass some more. I really never believed in fighting, but you can't live if you aren't able to defend yourself. I got better over the years.

One incident that may have helped my fighting skills was my rematch with the apparent descendent of the rooster who had raped me a few years back. Chickens, as you probably have figured out, were a common part of our rural life, both for food and, apparently, for entertainment. This was one mean bird, seeming to know just who or what might be afraid of him. Your local bird psychologist might say he was insecure and needed to prove his masculinity to the local hens. Well, based on my past record with roosters, I was terrified. When visiting next door, I had to peep out the door and around corners to make sure the coast was clear. If I wasn't sure, I'd get Uncle Ronald, a retired soldier, escort me. Since Ronald had spent time overseas, I figured he couldn't be afraid of a chicken. If he were, the country would have been in big trouble. When I think about it now, this is when I began to understand that this bully could be beaten. Watching my uncle tease the rooster with a board and showing no signs of fear must have registered at some level in my head. Nevertheless, I was still scared to death of that damn chicken. One day, after he had run me around the landscape a couple of times and across the stream, and as cousin Jeanette stood in the door laughing, something strange happened. My fear began to transform into a wave of pure anger, as I thought how ridiculous I must have looked. A thought shot through my head like a bolt of lightning. "I am sick and tired of this freaking chicken having control in my life and I am not going to take it anymore! We shall fight to the death—of one of us." My adrenalin was pumping and I prepared myself for major combat: **Ken Lineberry facing off with the World Champion of all chickens.** This was sure to be a barnburner. I broke stride and turned around to meet my fate. I wasn't going out without a fight. My instinct was to boot this fool to kingdom come. As he zeroed in for attack, I kicked at him, as if I were setting the all-time record for the longest field goal in NFL history. I closed my eyes and braced myself for impact. As my leg extended and followed through with this sure-to-be-deadly blow, I felt nothing but pure air. My thought was, "I have missed the fool and I'm going to die at the beak and claws of this mighty bird." I kept my eyes closed for a moment, so at least I wouldn't have to see all the blood and guts. I felt nothing. Slowly, I opened my eyes, and to my surprise, the rooster was walking away from me, as though his mission were over. I can hear him today, talking to himself in the voice of Mel Blanc's Foghorn Leghorn, "I say, I say boy, the boy finally got it. Yes, indeed he did." When it finished sinking in, I became ecstatic. I could not believe that I had spent weeks, maybe months, scared out of my wits by this bird, when all I ever needed to do was challenge him. It was that simple. That day, I cured my first patient, myself, of rooster phobia.

One morning, my mother asked me to chop the roosters head off so we could have him for dinner. I refused. I would rather have starved than kill a living creature intentionally. She took the axe and held it above the neck of my former enemy. I started to cry. I didn't hate or fear the rooster anymore. Actually, I think that, in a sense, I had bonded with him. Nevertheless, and after all we had gone through together, I watched him run around the back yard aimlessly, cutting flips without a head. Today, I believe that this big white rooster was sent by God to teach me an important lesson.

When I was in middle school, I instigated a fight with the school bully. He had interrupted my warm-up baseball throwing by talking to, and distracting, the other player. I threw the ball anyway, which almost hit the bully. What the hell was wrong with me? I figured that Eddie was gonna beat my ass. I was defiant. After all, I had at least one victory against Harold, another bully who picked on me the year before, and that triumph over the rooster.

Eddie approached and pushed me in the chest. I apologized for throwing the ball and told him I didn't want to fight. He pushed again and my flight-or-fight response kicked in, big time. I took off my Clark Kent eyeglasses, tossed them to the ground, removed my baseball glove, and imagined myself transformed into a young Cassius Clay. Eddie did not get in a single punch; I was on him like a tornado. The next thing I knew, he was on his back and I was straddling him and punching him in his bleeding mouth. Where had this monster come from? The next day, the news spread through school like wildfire. *Lineberry whipped Eddie's ass good!* Witnesses were illustrating the barrage of punches I had let lose on Eddie, a teacher intervened saying that fighting was nothing to be praised. Little did he know.

I did start to feel regret, mainly because I wasn't mad anymore. I was also afraid Eddie would tell one of his big brothers, star athletes, to take care of me. Nevertheless, the code of "fighting your own fights" held up and Kenneth Jay Lineberry went down in Siler City history for delivering one of the greatest ass-whippings a bully ever received. From this point forward, I realized that a monster lurked deep inside of me, a vicious monster, and I knew that I had to be careful never to let that monster loose again.

CHAPTER 3

Intro to Racism 101

Something Just Ain't Right Up in Here

Politics or social conditions were not a matter that concerned twelve year-old kids. I understand now that pep talk the class received from my favorite teacher, Mrs. Graves, when she kept emphasizing how we were going to be integrated with white students, and how imperative it was that we not let them exceed us academically. I was not really worried, because I had earned mostly A's and a few B's, without putting forth great effort. I had a reputation for being one of the most gifted students in the 5th grade. I realize now that this was 1969, shortly after the assassination of Martin Luther King, Jr. and Robert Kennedy. In those days, it was customary for kids to stay out of grown folks' conversations, so most of my peers and I were quite ignorant of current events. I had no idea what racism was; I had no concept of the hatred and hostility directed toward my people. I even remember driving through a Ku Klux Klan rally with my brother and his light-skinned wife and feeling confused, but not afraid. I had no idea how much danger we were in. However, being from Siler City, these Klansmen probably weren't associated with much open violence. When there were problems, like riots in the high schools, they were about things like changing the school name, Phantoms, to a something less offensive, such as Jets. My attitude was, simply, Why couldn't we all just get along?

The sixth grade began, and the first days were chaotic. The teachers knew very little about the students, so I was unfortunately placed in the low-IQ group. Eventually, they got it right and moved me to the intermediate group, which dampened my desire for learning...at least, that particular year. The only person who really seemed to give a damn was my mother, who became very upset if I didn't do well. Things were changing and I didn't understand why. I started to play Little League baseball that year and discovered that I could excel in something other than academics. I had already learned that I'd receive praise from more people if I did well.

This was also the time I had an encounter with another bully I refused to fight, despite his racial slurs and provocations.

But there was another problem ahead, which I couldn't see until later. Mr. Kenneth Elliott, the athletic director and overseer of all activities—and I do mean all— displayed a Confederate flag on the front bumper of his car and undoubtedly had a kind of Civil War Complex. He also loved to win. Eventually, it became clear that he did not want to see me succeed. The fact was that for one reason or another, there were many outstanding black athletes and very few, or hardly any, outstanding white ones. Would an openly racist coach use only his best athletes, who deserved to be a part of the team? If that happened, then the team could end up being predominantly black (or, heaven forbid, all black). If that happened, he'd have to face stiff condemnation at the PTA meetings...or any other gatherings. I can imagine what a problem this was for his psyche and easily imagine his line of thinking as: *"These jigs are trying to take over everything; I need to have as many white athletes as I can, but how? First, I need to get rid of as many blacks as possible. I'll save the cream of the crop and cut the rest, allowing me to have the best of both worlds."* Today, many conservative whites don't take into consideration that the idea of affirmative action is not new.

CHAPTER 4

Education in the Public Sector

I started the first grade in the fall of 1965, right during the peak of the civil rights movement. I had no concept of what the movement was and wouldn't even think seriously about it until my twenties. I remember that first day of school and my mother taking me into the classroom and leaving me in the custody of Mrs. Hanks. Mrs. Hanks was a thin black woman with protruding eyeballs. I didn't appreciate her for the great teacher she was until much later in life. In those days, teachers took no crap from students, period. Teachers of this era did not hesitate to make an example of any student who got out of line. They made sure everyone knew who was in control and a length of yardstick, paddleball paddles, even custom-made butt toasters were commonly used instruments of discipline. Mrs. Hanks specialized in the paddle, using the hyper-extended palm technique. It felt like needles sticking through your hand. Three licks was standard, but some offenses required five or more, until she tired of it. If the kid was unlucky, there was a sequel at home (if the parents found out).

I never took a paddling that seriously, if it were from a woman. Often times, I'd act out for the specific purpose of getting a paddling. Don't ask me why. (And notice I said as long as it was a woman giving the paddling!) Female teachers usually handled minor offenses, but if you really screwed up, you were sent to one of the male teachers or the principal. I *usually* had the good sense to not do anything bad enough to warrant that punishment. There was one time, however, when the teacher left the room and a couple of classmates and I thought we'd run around the chairs and cut up a little. We were taken to see Mr. Goldston. He took out that paddle and looked at us. We all started crying like babies. After a moment or two, he figured we had been punished enough and let us slide that time. On another occasion, the teacher's pet name-taker put my name down for accidentally dropping my pencil on the floor. For this, I received an undeserved paddling. I suppose that one was for the stuff I got away with. For all, there was a feeling of terror associated with one of those serious ass *whoopings*. Down the hallway, there was the wince producing sound of several loud slaps fired in rapid succession, sometimes followed by audible crying, imagining the sting, and then embarrassment the victim would feel from classmates. Everyone within hearing range was anxious to know who the unfortunate recipient was and soon the secret would be revealed. That level of punishment was not soon forgotten and was certainly deterrence from exhibiting certain behaviors. I know that there was...for me.

On that first day of school, the room was filled with six year-old kids. I'm sure we were all scared, never having been away from our homes for any significant amount of time. Some, like Thomasina, cried loudly, and everyday, for what seemed like an hour. I may have been anxious, but I knew it wasn't cool to be a crybaby. I had very little experience with girls at this time. A little girl, Poochi, visiting Johnny and Margie's house from Newport News, Va,. wanted me to play house with her and finally commandeered me. I remember that it was terrible. She made me lie in the chair, then she put lipstick on me and kept ordering me around. I think I would have preferred having the bully kick my ass. I got her back by standing outside the door and down the hallway a little, while her mother gave her a bath. She was terrified and crying that I was going to see her naked. I probably wouldn't have known what to look for, but at least I got some justice.

At school, I took an immediate liking to a cute girl sitting next to me. Her name was Suzette and I scoped her from head to toe, even found her sandaled feet mesmerizing! I looked at her so much that she had to keep telling the teacher to do something about me. At least I knew that being homesick would no longer be a problem for me, since the new object of my affection was what mattered most.

I had exceptional aptitude in the first grade. I could already do basic arithmetic, spell and write basic sentences. One day, Mrs. Hanks took me to a Third Grade teacher's and they had me do some arithmetic. They both were very impressed, but I thought little of it. It was clear that I was a gifted student. Were I in school today, however, I'm fairly certain that I'd be put on Ritalin. In retrospect, I see that I exhibited all kinds of daydreaming, poor concentration, restlessness and impulse control problems. Many times, I would sit in the back and write Suzette love letters. One day she told the teacher, who was a master of the disciplinary technique of backslapping (a method that would probably land a teacher in prison, if it were done today). The teacher demanded the letter and read it. I'm sure it was no more than *I love you. Do you love me? Please check Yes or No,* but there would be no checking that day: I had committed the crime of class disruption and would be sentenced to the usual punishment.

I always had a clowning nature, which some teachers didn't like, and this was one of them. As ordered, I assumed the position; she cocked her hand way back and began its forward motion. As her palm struck the upper mid-center of my back, I felt my breath leave my body, as if to tour the room before it returned. Promptly, the *"that didn't hurt"* face was activated. Of course, it hurt like hell.

I didn't write any more letters for a while.

In the second grade, I developed spells of nausea and had problems in class. It was eventually determined that I was blind as a bat and needed eyeglasses. Welcome to land of the Clark Kent nerds. My grandmother swore it was from staring into the TV set for hours, from point blank range. Nevertheless, I got glasses and it was so great to be able to see again. However, I felt it would be harder to win Suzette's affection, now that I was wearing bifocal Coke bottle lenses.

During that same year, I had to undergo an operation. I suffered from cryptorchidism, which simple means an undescended testicle. This was my first encounter with sickness and hospitalization. It also was a time when I felt most loved. My father took the time to take my mother and me to the hospital, which I now realize was extraordinary, given his circumstances. We stopped for a sandwich at a popular barbeque pit restaurant. At the hospital, my uncle Johnny and Margie brought me fruit and a Batman toy. I didn't really know what all this meant because I felt fine. When everyone left, I buzzed the nurse every five minutes for little or no reason. She set the limits right away. I awakened the next day feeling horrible, and with an enormous bandage around my lower abdomen and waist. What the hell had they done to me? I learned to be a brave patient and made a complete recovery.

The third grade was a pretty good year and I remember learning about science and math, as well as songs from the hit play and movie, *The Sound of Music.* We had a party for Christmas and were told to bring records. I brought my sister's 45RPM of the Rolling Stones' *Get Off Of My Cloud* and *I Can't Get No Satisfaction.* I also loaned my favorite album, *Alvin and the Chipmunks,* to a classmate and never saw it again. My Cub Scout pack had their party and exchanged gifts, and I got some clay. I was elated, because I could make things with it. The most important event occurred afterward, as I waited for my ride home. Suzette was also waiting and, eventually, we were alone. I don't know what happened, but nice words flowed from me and she reciprocated. I couldn't believe she was treating me so nicely. My body must have been releasing tons of endorphins because it felt as though I were floating on a cloud. What a wonderful feeling! Now that she finally liked me, what was next? I had just turned nine, so that ruled out picking her up in my Corvette for a date. At that age, we knew nothing of intimacy or romance. So there was really nothing to do but laugh at each other's weak jokes and hope the feeling lasted. Five months later, she transferred to another school. Having conquered that feeling of failing to win this girl's approval was blissful. Unfortunately, it was also fleeting.

My Fourth Grade was Mrs. Moore, a tall, lean, auburn-headed woman with pronounced contractures of one hand, probably due to some form of nerve disease. She had a reputation for putting up with very little and swinging a mean stick. Her paddle was custom designed and had a list of autographs from past victims. Mrs. Moore scared me almost as much as the male teachers, especially after I witnessed her in action, turning the seat of one boy's brown corduroy pants from dark brown to light tan. I must have been masochistic, because I felt destined to get my name on that paddle. I can't recall what I did, but I do recall two or three paddlings that year. All I remember is that sting-on-the-butt feeling, as though a nest of bumblebees had decided to test their stingers simultaneously. Since I was now an experienced lady's man (from my fifteen minutes of romancing Suzette), it was destiny that I not let this talent go to waste. I was approaching age eleven, so I couldn't waste a lot of time. I think it was that spring when I met Patsy. Aunt Margie had been invited over by Mrs. Price to pick some cherries and I was along for the ride. Patsy was a pretty brown-skinned girl who was as nice and sweet as she was attractive. I picked up exactly where I had left off with the first love of my life and we sat together on the swing, engaged in deep conversation about absolutely nothing. I remember the euphoria, as though you want the moment to continue forever. I was profoundly infatuated, but believed that this was love. I had found my queen! But now what? What probably happened was that I entered a fantasy world in which I would soothe myself from unpleasantness and where reality paled in comparison. This behavior was not healthy for me and, when my fantasy world later collided with reality, would lead to embarrassment or guilt.

I was becoming addicted to these love fantasies, which I now believe served the purpose of filling the void left from not having a regular father in my life. All of this is, of course, retrospective analysis: at that age, I was unable to think with such logic.

My main concern was being sure to see Patsy on the bus, at choir practice, or wherever possible. She was a grade ahead of me, so I rarely saw her at school. One cold wintry day, as it was preparing to snow, her dad offered me a ride from choir practice to my uncle's. The three of us rode together in the pickup truck and the ride lasted perhaps three minutes, but I was ecstatic for those minutes. It was as though I were on a wonderful date both in my mind and my heart. Patsy was the greatest thing to happen to me, I felt at the time. Even though we clearly liked each other, the relationship existed primarily in my mind, which was not healthy. It was not unlike one might imagine cocaine use. While the high lasts, it is the greatest thing in the world, but when it wears off, the dysphoria is greater and lasts longer than the brief pleasure. It wasn't time to pay the piper yet; for the time being, I had my wonderful romantic fantasies.

The Fifth Grade came and it was a very good year. I adored my teacher, Mrs. Graves, and was one of her favorite students. My grades were outstanding and I loved school. I remember looking at a book that included a section on human anatomy. I thought the male and female reproductive organs were interesting, which made some of the female students consider me somewhat weird. Actually, I just had a very healthy curiosity. During this year, Patsy remained queen, although she was going steady with Mrs. Grave's son, Craig. I had fun playing around with several of the girls in the classroom and on the school bus, but the feelings were nothing like those I felt with my first two girlfriends.

I'm not conceited or arrogant, but the opposite sex has always been naturally attracted to me. This eventually developed into a problem because I never learned the proper way to pursue or initiate a relationship. Or, for that matter, to maintain a relationship. I've always had problems with assertiveness in terms of relating to women, which naturally leads to attracting a more aggressive type of woman. This can only lead to problems. Therefore, missed opportunities and failed relationships have been my trademark.

At age ten, however, this was not an issue.

As the year progressed, auditions were held for the yearly production. This year, it happened to be *The Wizard of Oz,* a movie that fascinated me. There was a special woman directing the production, a white woman, which was new for most of us. I won the role of the tin man and looked forward to rehearsals. My costume was composed of cardboard boxes and aluminum foil. The audience went wild, seeing schoolmates playing those familiar characters and the chorus singing such memorable tunes. I loved being on stage and interacting with the audience. Acting was something I was good at and something I might have enjoyed doing for the rest of my life. However, it wasn't in the cards for me and, after that production, it had to take a back seat to academics and eventually sports. It sure was fun while it lasted!

CHAPTER 5

Adolescence

Play Your Hand

I t was 1970 and a new decade was beginning. Chatham High School, known as the colored or Negro school for grades one through twelve, became Chatham Middle School, now a newly integrated middle school for grades six through eight. Just as Mrs. Graves had told us, we now had white classmates and there would be no more special attention from teachers.

My teacher this year, was a stocky brunette on whom I developed a crush. She wore stockings and short skirts, and I loved to sit at the front of the class. My only memory about academics that year was the new grading system: Poor/Satisfactory/Outstanding.

I joined the band and began to learn the trumpet, even I earned a few merit badges in the Boy Scouts. I also tried out for Little League and won the starting position in left field. This was my first encounter with organized sports. I was a very good defensive player and slightly better than average at the plate. That summer was a crucial and painful time in my young life because Aunt Margie died of pancreatic cancer. This was both shocking and disconcerting because she was the first person close to me to die. I didn't realize it then, but life would never be the same.

By the seventh grade, I was fairly accustomed to all of the changes; being a good student was no longer a top priority. I was developing an interest in sports and learning about our local high school heroes , and such sports stars as , Walt "Clyde" Frazier, Gene Washington, Johnny Unitas, Frank Robinson, , Muhammad Ali, and countless other great athletes. It seemed more reasonable to emulate these figures than to study math and science. During our Sunday afternoon games with all the neighborhood kids, I was a star of football, basketball, and baseball. In my mind, that made me the epitome of greatness and gave me the opportunity to not only dream about, but actually be, that favorite star for a short while. My backyard, where most of our sporting events took place, was the scene of competition that was often fierce. Occasionally, a scuffle or two would break out. I sometimes dressed in my Sears and Roebuck special football uniform, which took the fantasy to a higher level. The other players were usually my age or a little older. My cousin, Al, who was four years older, felt obliged to take it easy on us. One Sunday, I believed that my team was being cheated and I got angry. With that anger, my fear of tackling Al went away and I led a goal-line stand that prevented him from scoring a touchdown. Now, scoring was routine for him, since his size advantage meant he could turn it on and off as he saw fit. But there was no touchdown this time. This time, that response once used to defeat a rooster was used once again, only this time on a big guy. This is when I learned that anger could be very useful.

It was time to put some of this great talent to use for the Chatham Middle School Rams, so I went out for the football team. After a few weeks of grueling practice in the hot August sun, I was informed that my services were no longer needed. I realized how bad it felt to fail at something that you really wanted. I played in a league at the city park that year, instead of for the school. The coaching was not very good and it was not much fun. I think I played defensive end and offensive guard and saw pretty minimal playing time, except for practice. I played basketball for the Lakers (we all had names of professional teams) and I was one of the better players, which made it fun.

When spring came, I decided to try out for the baseball

team. I did well in tryouts, until I broke my glasses. My eyesight was terrible, so I was dropping balls and couldn't see well enough to hit the ball. Did the coach care about my glasses being broken? Hell no! He sent my ass packing without a second thought, so I played Pony league and finished up hitting well and being a competent outfielder.

In the classroom, I did enough to get by: I was not motivated when it came to academics. I could have made all A's, but I saw no reason to spend the time and effort required to do that. Moreover, Suzette had returned and I passed much of my time sending messages through her cousin about how much I liked her. I was insanely crazy about her...until I saw her in person. The problem was that when I was around her and had the opportunity to back up some of the bravado, I became paralyzed and mute, and felt like running away and hiding. I could tell that she liked me, too, but I was never able to bring myself around to saying a single word to her. I'm sure it appeared as though I were ignoring her and I quickly learned that the worse thing you can do to a girl is ignore her. I was really quite pitiful.

I learned that this fantasy thing just does not match up with reality. In my youthful fantasies, I was Casanova and Don Juan. In reality, however, I was a total embarrassment to myself. I no longer had the ability to make simple conversation. The worst part was that this only applied to the person I was crazy about. If I had no romantic feelings for a girl, I had no trouble whatsoever saying whatever crossed my mind. But in the case of Suzette and Patsy, it was over. As much as I idolized them, it was as though I were under general anesthesia, but with my eyes and ears open, but totally incapable of responding. Patsy eventually faded away and became involved with other boys. Suzette made a few attempts at making me jealous by pretending to like other guys in my presence until she decided it wasn't worth the trouble. She then became an agent to help one of her friends, in whom I had zero interest, hook up with me. That, too, was futile.

As I said, I had no problem with girls for whom I had

no deep feelings. A problem occurred only if I started to like them. And remember, I had no knowledge of intimacy or sexual relations at this time, although most girls seemed to see something in me. I made friends with three white girls and we played around, but it was nothing serious. One of the girls said that she wanted my weenie, but I was clueless, which was a good thing. Another commented that, if I were white, she would love to be my girlfriend. I couldn't tell if that was a compliment or a putdown. Looking back, it was probably an indicator of how race relations had taught thirteen year- olds to view the world.

Unfortunately, I was already dealing with some serious issues, in regards to how I was perceived. This was a form of inferiority complex: I was filled with shame, as well as little or no pride. I was ashamed of not having a father; I was ashamed of being poor; I was ashamed of the old house we lived in. I was also ashamed of having to depend on others for transportation, ashamed of my nerdy Clark Kent glasses, and ashamed of not having the ability to say what I wanted to the girls I liked, who I felt gave me pleasure. I felt as though I had nothing and others had everything. When I got on or off the bus, I always came from, or went to, Jeannette's house. It was a pretty brick house, not like the one I lived in, which was old and ugly, and symbolic of how I was thinking of myself. I stopped wearing my glasses, choosing blindness over appearing eccentric or unattractive. I can still over hear Suzette in the background exclaiming, "*Why don't that boy wear his glasses, he know he can't see?*" I even became ashamed of eating certain foods. I went on a pinto been strike, which had always been one of my favorite foods.

Needless to say, at this point in my life, I was very unhappy, lost, and confused. I had no idea of what was important and there was no one to work with me there or teach me. I recall the spelling bee in which I was a finalist. I didn't even want to win. I'm certain that this dampened my effort because I felt more relief than upset when I finally misspelled a word. For one thing, I didn't like this feeling of responsibility placed on me, having to defend the fact I was black. At least, by this time, I had graduated the identities of colored and Negro! So what if the winner was a white girl? I didn't care, yet the teacher hoped that I'd win. Had I understood the significance then, as I do now, I suppose I would have tried harder.

The Chi-Lites sang *Oh Girl* and *Have You Seen Her?*, while Three Dog Night belted the lyrics to *Joy to the World* as the Eighth Grade got underway. Things began to change a little. For starters, I made the football team as a defensive back. Practice was more fun, and one day during scrimmage I even picked off a Barney Siler pass and took it fifty yards, only to be caught from behind and tackled on the one-yard line by James Siler. (no relation.) Remember, I was living in Siler City! In retrospect, that single play represented my athletic strengths and weaknesses. As a boy and as a young man, I was blessed with feline-quick reflexes and unusual hand and finger dexterity. The previous year, during a class softball game, Greg Headen (no relation) hit a line drive to left field, which I was playing much too shallow. As the ball came off the bat, I saw that it was well hit and turned instantly to sprint toward the area where the trajectory would send the ball. Had I been a cat in another life I would have been a lion because I was extremely quick over the first few yards, yet I lacked the ability to accelerate at the end, like all great sprinters. Lions are like that: if they do not snag the prey quickly, they will tire and the gazelle will be spared, leaving the big cat frustrated and hungry. A cheetah, on the other hand, has a quick takeoff coupled with continued acceleration and stamina, allowing it to sustain speeds of nearly sixty mph, and for an impressive amount of time. The lion must therefore have excellent instincts, strategy, and skills in order for it and the pride to survive.

Without further digression: The ball left the bat, I aligned myself with its path, and then sprinted perhaps twenty to thirty yards, when the adrenaline kicked in. With my left arm fully extended, and never breaking stride, and my internal calculators interpolating perfectly, my feet left the ground and the ball landed directly into my palm. I braced myself for the crash landing, but it turned out to be equally as graceful. It was as if, in that split second, I had been transformed into a person with unlimited human abilities. From that day on Mr. Edwards who was, both the PE teacher and assistant coach, referred to me as Claw Lineberry. He even made up a story about the legend of the claw, which he presented to the class. I blushed immensely and hoped that the coach would hear of this feat and select me for the baseball team.

As a boy growing up under these particular circumstances, it was important to find ways of boosting one's self esteem or self worth, in order to defend against the negative influences of the world, both the country and the community. Sports were beginning to play this esteem-building role in my life. Had it not been for sports, I hate to think where all the anger, feelings of shame, and penned-up frustrations may have led me.

During this school year, there was so much talent and limited positions that they decided to form two basketball teams, the A-team and B–team. I made the first few cuts and began to feel that this might be my year. Disappointingly, I did not survive the last cut. That really hurt, but I rationalized that it was for the best: I had no transportation. My sense of defeat was somewhat assuaged when, during an intramural game, I sunk a last-second shot from midcourt. I couldn't help thinking that my luck might change! I tried out for the volleyball team, but ran into the usual problem of being overlooked to allow an acceptable racial balance, and again was informed that my services were not required. I could have thrown in the towel, but I'm too stubborn for that, so I went out for tumbling.

Tumblers were known for their half-time events during basketball games. It was impossible to be cut from the tumbling team! However, with Coach Elliott in charge, it was hard to know what to expect. I am not sure what I was thinking, but I gave that tumbling my all. And although it isn't the most masculine sport, I think I enjoyed the tumbling events more than I would have bench-riding with the basketball team. Then again, maybe that's sour grapes. I do know that tumbling taught me to feel good about what I do, no matter what it is.

Spring approached, the weather warmed, and I got ready for baseball tryouts, the fear of being cut weighing heavily on me. I had new glasses, so Elliott couldn't use that against me. And yet I knew deep down that if Elliott could find any reason, I was gone.

I busted my ass to challenge his reluctance to treat me fairly. I caught every fly ball, fielded every grounder, threw and hit well, and never let up. My confidence was boosted because I had previously won my Pony League starting spot and the Pitch, Hit, and Throw competition. My attitude was clearly: practice makes perfect. Now I had to deal with this bigoted coach.

About a week into practice, my friend Keith, who was a favorite of the coach, complimented me and said that, if I continued my current hustle and effort, I was sure to make the team. I always liked Keith and respected his skills as an athlete and a leader. Tragically, Keith was stabbed to death at the age of thirty-two, an event of even greater tragedy because his older brother died of tick fever several years earlier. I felt badly for his family.

Again, I have digressed. It was just as Keith had said and I made the baseball team! It was a very good season for me because I was a starter and played well in most games. It felt so good to be one of the boys again. Even if I wasn't much of a talker, sports were one place where I could express many things and feel worthwhile amongst my peers. Academics never offered such comradery. In fact, academics had become little more than a requirement to play sports. And sports is where I found role models. Remember that these were the days when nobody was putting great emphasis on a college future. In the romance department that year, thoughts of Suzette and Patsy faded and I became attracted to a 7th grader named Sylvia. There was just something about her appearance that I really liked. Don Juan Casanova was back and ready to sweep the lady off her feet— even if it was only in his mind! This obsessing over an object of affection was becoming an entrenched part of my psyche that I felt unable to change, even if I desired to. Sylvia was in the band and in my PE class. Eventually she got the message of my interest. Of course, I had no clue as to why I wanted to be with her or what I was supposed to do. This was bound to cause some problems. Every time I saw her, I got butterflies in my stomach, knots in my throat, and then I blushed and become deaf, dumb and mute. It never failed and I always felt badly afterward. Away from her, I was comfortable talking to people about almost anything. Around her, I couldn't think well enough to develop a sentence, and though initially elated, the feeling eventually became utter embarrassment, as though I were frontrunner for the Dunce of the Year Contest. I continued to return for more punishment. The thing that made it so hard was that the girl actually liked me. In fact, we adored each other, but I was much shyer and that made it so awkward whenever we saw each other. I think I smashed the volleyball into her head once, in PE. That earned me lots of points! However, she continued to choose me as her square dance partner. Yes, square dancing in PE class. Whether square dancing was popular with the brothers or not, I didn't care in the least; it was a chance to be close to Sylvia and she was the all that mattered to me. I felt as though I were in heaven for those few minutes. That is, until the time came to actually talk to her, and then my tongue became tied. I had no idea what to say to her. I was in heaven and hell at the same time.

One day, a fellow student Eric, told me that Sylvia was his girlfriend and that I should back off. This type of thing was common among the young males who liked the same girl. He told me he'd been rapping to her, was once her boyfriend, and he wanted her back. He was actually a good sport, though a bit cocky, yet we liked each other. He told me that she was going to announce her choice at a certain time on the following day.

The next day was gloomy, with light rain. My competition asked me to walk with him and his friend, a top athlete, to his house to pick up something and I complied. Much of the time he taunted me about he was the person Sylvia belonged with. Later, I received the news that Eric was the chosen one from Eric, and I was devastated. My interpersonal skills with girls were so underdeveloped and my self esteem was so deficient that I just accepted his word, feeling as though I didn't deserve to be with her. I backed away for a while. Of course, it turned out that Eric wasn't with her and she liked me as much as ever. She gave me a few more chances at ball games and at the pool. She even faked interest in a guy to make me jealous. All I could do well was play ball, not talk. I knew I was the worst talker in the history of heterosexual relationships. That self image eventually filtered through and she stopped wasting her time with such an emotionally impaired individual. I kept the thoughts of her in my mind for days to come. (The fantasy version is almost always superior to the reality version.) I may have appeared perfectly fine on the exterior, but inside I was dying, and not quite sure why. To the now nostalgic sounds of The O'Jays' *Love Train*, The Four Tops' *Ain't No Woman Like the One I Got* and The Cornelius' Bros and Sister Rose's *Too Late to Turn Back Now*, Middle School eventually ended with mixed emotions.

I began to wonder what high school was going to be like.

CHAPTER 6

Up-rooted

Everything Happens for a Reason

Over the summer of '73, Al Green became my lifelong favorite performer. In August, I began my freshman year at Jordan Matthews High School. At age fourteen, this was the big time. Since I was in the marching band and assigned a new instrument, the baritone horn, I decided to sit out junior varsity football and focus entirely on making the basketball team, the one sport in which I had failed to make the school team. I had read a book by Gale Goodrich of the Lakers, which inspired me, so I committed myself to making the team. When I got home in the afternoons, I ran through the woods for about a mile, jumped some rope, and shot baskets until dark. My strategy was to be so good I couldn't be cut. There were about twenty-five others trying out for JV basketball. The initial practices were mixed, with varsity players included, until football season ended. This was exciting, but I was scared of failing, which made me work harder on my own. I remembered how Elliott had cut me from the 8th grade team and that gave me extra motivation. I couldn't understand why I had been cut and was afraid it would happen again. I vowed that if I didn't succeed, it would not be due to lack of effort. I knew that coaches loved hustle and I believed I could hustle with the best of them.

Kermit *(another Siler-ite)* was my buddy since early

childhood. His father, James, took us to and from practice, so I didn't have to worry about transportation. That is, until Kermit was cut from the squad. I was willing to walk the three miles, if there was no other recourse. But it was stressful, not knowing how I'd get home. Nevertheless, I had never let that stop me in the past and I sure wasn't going to now. Even when people saw me walking and offered a ride, I refused. I had my pride. I sometimes walked along the railroad track, desperately hoping that no one I knew would see me. I was really angry at my mother because we had no car and I vowed that, if and when I became an adult, I would never be in a position where I had to depend on others for anything.

My pride was quite foolish at times and caused me to do stupid things, like sit in the rain for three hours when I forgot my ticket money for a Varsity basketball game. I could have borrowed it, or worked out something with the gatekeeper, but not me. In the same vein, I turned down rides that would have had me home in five minutes, only to avoid feeling like a charity case. I had many conversations with myself, while walking down those tracks.

I made the freshman team, which got to dress out with the JV team, which started the season with a perfect record. Whenever the JV's blew out an opponent, "the scrubs" (as we sometimes referred to the benchwarmers) would see some action. I remember the first lay-up I made in a real game. It was really exciting and felt so good to finally be one of the basketball boys. I loved going on the game trips. My hard work had finally paid off.

Sitting outside one day after practice, my old friend Mr. Elliott, the Athletic Director from the middle school came by. Of course, he asked me what I was doing there and I was delighted to tell him that I was just getting out of basketball practice. That closed my chapter with him for good: I no longer needed his help to believe in my abilities.

Fate is weird sometimes. I saw Elliott as my adversary, but he turned out to be the person who introduced me to Sigmund Freud and Psychology, one of his passions. Also, his attitude taught me to push myself to the maximum. Much like my earlier friend, the rooster, Elliott helped me attain a higher level that would not have been attainable without him. I owe a lot of my success to him. I forgive him for those times he treated me unfairly and I accept that everything played out was designed to be part of the grand scheme of my life.

December rolled around and I sensed something was changing at home, but I wasn't sure what. I knew that my mother was seeing my father again and that she was gone for periods of time. She seemed to be less concerned about home: sometimes there was no dinner and the refrigerator was empty, which was unusual. I helped keep the fire in the wood heater going, so Mama and I could stay warm.

Bringing in wood was my number one chore. Most of the time, I'd be in the living room playing electric football with Gary or Jimmy or practicing alone with my plastic men. I had hand-painted many of them and was especially proud of my 49ers and Rams. One good thing was that my sister Alfreda planned to visit for the holidays from Baltimore. She always brought me something I wanted or needed. This year, she was bringing me a stereo.

Alfreda was the first in my family to finish college. She graduated from North Carolina Central University in the late 1960's, a predominantly black school, and was a schoolteacher. She was a major influence, advising me academically and socially, and another person who made my life turn out so well.

I usually took my vacations visiting Baltimore. It was a real treat playing stickball in the street with Cousin Tony and Tina and their cast of friends. It was also a special treat to watch the Orioles play baseball. Uncle Van was not very good about showing affection, but he always gave us money. Aunt Edna was a great cook.

I was so glad to see Alfreda get out of the cab on that one Friday night. But the following morning I awakened to hear a loud conversation in the kitchen. Later, Alfreda came into my bedroom and asked if I were aware that Ruth was planning to marry Otis and move from Siler City to Goldston. This came as a shock and I found myself starting to weep. Ruth came in and sat on my bed, trying to comfort me by telling me how things would be better and that Otis and his 12-year-old son, Earl, were looking forward to me being a part of their family.

The most important thing in my life was that basketball team and there was no way I'd let that go, especially after all the effort I put into making the team. When I finally told my friends that I wouldn't be around anymore, they were shocked. I was willing to move in with Uncle Johnny next door, since Jeanette had married and moved to Greensboro. However, it was made clear to me that I was expected to move to Goldston. Through my basketball, I had fought feelings of depression and had finally accepted my fate. I was hoping to find a way to continue at my school, but it became clear that this was not going to work.

Mama moved to Winston Salem to stay with her oldest daughter. I usually went back to the empty house, shot baskets in the mud, and then caught a cab back to the school for practice. I wasn't aware that Johnny had been diagnosed with cancer and that my good-bye to him was to be our final good-bye. There was just too much happening. Why couldn't life be simple and let me play my basketball and not have to be concerned about all these changes?

Our next game was against Chatham Central in Bear Creek. This was the school to which I was to eventually be transferred. We beat their JV team by about 40 points that night, but for some reason the coach chose not to let me play. After the game, I didn't ride the bus back to Siler City because Bear Creek was only three miles from my new home. I was waiting outside the gym for my ride and Mr. Scott, my future football coach, started asking questions about me being there. It was a conference violation for me to play for Jordan Matthews, since I no longer lived in that school district, meaning I had to accept letting go all that I had worked so hard for.

I had no idea of what to expect at my new school, but it was now inevitable that I could not remain at Jordan Matthews. Par for the course, it rained during my first day, as I got on the school bus headed for Central. My stop was near the end of the route, so there were only a few seats left. I was nervous, but I've always had the ability to hide that when necessary.

When I started at my new school, I knew only a few people, but making friends was not a major problem. I met Tim, who would be a co-guard with me when we won the first ever JV championship at Central. I also met Danny a.k.a. Frank, who would become an all- conference quarterback and lead us to the best two seasons in the school's history. I met John, the principal's son, who would one day be head coach for the varsity basketball team at my old high school. There was also, Chris, who became a very close friend. Eventually, he grew like a tree and learned to dunk the ball. Later, he also replaced me as a starter on the varsity team. Melvin was another friend. He had his own car and was in band with Chris and me. He also played football and basketball. My first day, I loaned a kid named LT my tennis shoes for PE. He went on to become one of the biggest bums in Goldston history. Chatham Central was a smaller school than my former school, and it had the advantage of there being no real strangers. The disadvantage, sports-wise, was the smaller pool of athletes. On the positive side, however, was that I attained instant recognition. I began suiting up with the freshman basketball team. The team left a bit to be desired, but with me, they looked more like a team and were more competitive in most of the games that remained. I had perfected my set and jump shots and made about 70% of them, plus 90% of my free throws. We weren't winning, but my talent was finally under the spotlight and it felt great. We played my old freshman team and I really wanted to win this one. I scored in double figures, but couldn't sink a free throw for anything, missing at least three. We lost by one point and I really felt bad, but the game allowed me to earn some respect from Mr. Craven, my future varsity coach. I was a strong prospect for JV for the next year.

I finished up the school year going out for baseball. I made the team easily, which was destined to be North Carolina State 2A champions in 1976. I was the only minority on the squad and it sometimes seemed—by off-the-cuff comments and frequent racial slurs—that some of my teammates either had no regard for my feelings or just forgot that I was black. My hitting had improved tremendously and I actually hit a few homeruns and batted in the cleanup position.

My father, Otis, never actually said so, but I knew he was proud that I played on the team. Subliminally, the ball and glove he had bought for me at age four must have influenced my interest in baseball. He went as far as to watch us practice from afar one day. This was uncommon for him because he had never established a comfortable means of communicating with me, and he really hated picking me up after any event. He never even acknowledged having been there. In a perfect world, he would have waited until practice ended and I would have ridden home and held a conversation about what he had witnessed.

In retrospect, I now understand that Otis was clueless about what being a father was all about. There were two boys, Mike and Ronnie, who did most of their growing up with his first wife in Washington, D.C. I never met either of these half brothers. Ronnie was shot to death two years later, at the age of twenty-seven, and I attended his funeral, but my introduction to him was with him lying in a casket. To this day, I have never met his brother, Michael. I know that Otis felt something for them, and it was unfortunate that he couldn't build a relationship with either of them. He did seem a little disturbed when he told me that Ronnie was killed, as if I had known him well. I met his ex–wife, Beatrice, while attending their son's funeral. Although she was approaching sixty years of age, she was a strikingly attractive woman with a warm personality. At least that's the impression she gave me. Otis never talked about her or what happened when they were a family. I got the sense that the marriage was rather short and disappointing. It wasn't difficult to see why things turned out the way that they did.

As I got to know Otis better over the years, I identified some of the traits that we have in common: narcissism; difficulty building deep relationships. As a narcissist, he was consumed by self-admiration and felt special, often blinded to the emotional needs of others, except in certain crises. Some of his childhood friends, even into adulthood, referred to Otis as Toddler, because of his delay in maturity as a child, I assumed. At a superficial level, he was great at dealing with people, but he had major problems bonding with loved ones. I still struggle with that trait, with bonding and building satisfying and comfortable relationships with those to whom I am closest. It's as though a transparent partition exists between the person and me. Imagine what a double partition would be like, when father and son communicate with each other.

The local guys were planning to bring baseball back to Goldston the upcoming summer with a new version of the White Sox. A meeting for interested parties was held at Otis' Barbershop, which had a tradition of being the place to go when in Goldston. You could say it was like the black folks' version of Floyds' Barber Shop in Mayberry, on the Andy Griffith Show. The meeting was held, and I must say that Otis made it clear that I had played for the high school and should be part of the team. This sounded attractive to me, because on the high school team, I never really felt welcome, and there was the feeling of being intimidated, due to lack of advocacy or support. Therefore, I bid farewell to Chatham Central baseball team. Jackie Robinson had already dealt with the color issue and I was not willing to play a scaled-down country version of his plight.

CHAPTER 7

The Pendulum Swings Both Ways

My sophomore year came and I felt rather sophomoric! I decided to try out for Junior Varsity football. The varsity team was having a rebuilding year and had taken the best sophomore players, so neither the JV nor the Varsity had a solid team. I had developed a work ethic of giving a 101% and had no problem making the team. I felt euphoria about being a starter. I had never experienced this and still bore the perceived scars from my experience in middle school.

My self-confidence was at an all time high. Retrospectively, I now see that sports were my coping mechanism through which I dissipated my internal rage in an acceptable way, through the process of sublimation. Unfortunately, the price I paid was that my self worth and identity became attached to how well I performed on the field or court. I developed a need to repeatedly prove my worth, partially because my appearance was more that of a scholar than an athlete. This type of behavior is difficult to change.

The JV season began and there were a few discoveries that surprised even me. My ability to run with the football turned out to be phenomenal. At that time, OJ Simpson was at his peak and people often told me that my running style was similar to his. It was like, when I got that football in my hand, I felt invincible and refused to be stopped. My foot speed had developed even further and my psychomotor skills were superb. I was able to fake out would-be tacklers, and could spin off a defensive player while barely breaking stride. It was always exciting when I got the football. My biggest weakness continued to be the inability to shift into that last gear and accelerate to the goal line. For the first thirty yards, however, I could hang with the best of them. I was blessed with a graceful quickness, like the lion (as I previously mentioned), but the acceleration and stamina of the cheetah is required to put the finishing touch on a good run. With that ability, I would have been unstoppable. I returned several kickoffs for thirty or forty yards and had several long runs from scrimmage, even caught a couple of nice passes, but I didn't have the breakaway acceleration that separates a good running back from a great running back. I usually made up for it with heart, and the refusal to be taken down. After seeing my performance, the coach immediately moved me to the varsity team, where one of the backs had suffered a knee injury. I wasn't sure if I was ready for this. Three years prior, I couldn't even make the team; now I'm being considered as a possible starter. This seemed like divine intervention, making up for those times I'd been treated unfairly, and not objectively. There had to be such a thing as karma. Things were starting to look promising.

There is one thing that's been hard for men of color to avoid, and that's racism raising its ugly head. Because there were to be only a handful of blacks on the team, some of the same guys from the previous year's baseball team would be blocking for me. Clearly, the better they did their job, the better I was going to look. I imagine this is quite a dilemma for any teammate who has racial prejudices. It was my hope that the drive to be a winner would help us bond and that foolishness would not be a factor.

We ended that season with a 2-8 record, losing a heartbreaker in the last game to North Moore. It had been a tough-fought battle, with the opponent up 7-0 going into the fourth quarter. We finished our last drive with a touchdown pass and had the option of kicking the extra point for a tie, or going for two points and the win. Coach decided "What the hell, let's go for the victory!" Unfortunately, not even our All Conference receiver, Darryl T., could save us this time. The 1974 season ended when the pass to the end zone was incomplete.

Sports had clearly become my escape and my refuge from much of the unpleasantness in my life, though at the time I had no idea that this was the real role it played. I was feeling grief about abandoning my birthplace—every foot of that property was etched in my mind for as far back as I could remember. I loved to play in the little stream catching minnows, crawfish, tadpoles, even a baby snake or two. Except for walking by the cows, I loved wandering along the paths in the woods on my way to choir practice or to visit my cousins. Once I had moo'ed at the cows, causing them to run toward me (they thought I had their lunch!). They couldn't jump the fence, but I was still terrified to walk by them. I also missed my imaginary sports arena, where whatever sport was in season was played on Sundays after church.

Within a few months, I moved into a new setting, one totally foreign to me and with a whole new cast of characters. Retrospectively, and with a bit of therapy and independent reflection, it all makes more sense to me now. The home situation was extremely bad, though I never spoke to anyone about it. I think this is when I began to try to resolve or deal with my problems alone. I felt as if there was no one to go to.

My new brother, Earl, had lost his mother to cancer a few years prior to Otis remarrying my mother. Otis had pretty much dealt with Earl's grief by buying him whatever he wanted or caving in to his every demand, no matter how silly. Since his mother was no longer there to carry on the pampering and spoiling, it fell to Otis. There were stories of Earl slapping Otis in the face for refusing him something, and this was while Otis was cutting a customer's hair. In effect, an emotional aberration had been allowed to develop. When Earl found out that Otis was my biological father, all bets were off. He declared an all-out passive aggressive campaign to make my life unbearable and sabotage any peace or happiness in the home. Earl learned early on that he was no match for me, from a physical standpoint. On occasion, he taunted me with a vast array of profane and disgusting names, but I usually ignored him for as long as I could. I was extremely tolerant of much of his mischief.

The first time that I lost my patience, it was when I had pleaded for him to stop harassing me but he only did it more. I had tried my best never to let that monster come out again, but sometimes you just can't help it. One evening, we were walking up to the barbershop with a couple of neighborhood kids and he pushed the wrong button by taunting me. I felt rage swell up and adrenalin warm me all over. The next thing I remember, I was stomping him on the ground like a cockroach. From then on, he realized that making me angry was not in his best interest.

In retrospect, what Earl needed was some fatherly intervention and diplomacy. Unfortunately, that was not a possibility. Following that incident, Earl used more covert means of attack, such as throwing my eyeglasses and baseball glove into a field and then pretending to know nothing about it. He gave away many of my possessions, including my model football men, my BB gun, and items of clothing. Anytime something was missing, I expected to find it with a neighbor kid or thrown away. Once, Earl set my shirt on fire while I was asleep in the chair. Fortunately, I awakened in time to douse it out before being burned. Needless to say, he denied knowing what happened.

Earl engaged in other misbehavior around the house: eating or giving away our desert before anyone had any; making a mess of all the rooms; urinating on the toilet seat and floor; plus countless other nuisance-like acts. He knew that all he had to do was deny it and nothing more was said. He didn't even take Otis seriously. This made me steam inside, but it wasn't my place to discipline him.

As for Otis, he spent all of his time at the barbershop and poolroom next door to it, so he never got involved with anything at the house. I always tried to avoid having to witness Earl disrespect my mother, mainly because I knew I wouldn't be able to control my response

That Christmas, Otis asked me to go with him to help

pick out an electric guitar for Earl, although I don't remember receiving any significant gift for myself. There were many times when I wished I had stayed in Siler City with Johnny. The youth community in Goldston seemed so unwelcoming.

One Sunday, we were playing in the poolroom and Earl went outside, where Ruth and Otis had just pulled up. When he returned, I asked what they wanted and he said, "Nothing, just to tell me that somebody named Johnnie died." He said this in a very disrespectful and uncaring manner. Johnny had been my father figure as a child and I was shocked to learn of his passing.

Earl carried on in that spirit for years to come and I continued trying to avoid him whenever possible. He spent most of his time lying on the living room sofa watching TV, never bathing or combing his hair. He was a very talented artist and would draw all day. There was only one other time, a few years later, when he provoked me into whipping his ass and making it clear that I would never again allow him to disrespect me, my mother, or my grandmother. Otis heard about it and sent a neighborhood teenager of my age to deal with the situation. Earl retaliated by using a razor to cut up my Sunday suit coat and my favorite yearbook

I know now that what Earl needed was some tough love, and for Otis to show that he cared in ways other than providing material things. I was actually raised pretty well and, although I wanted a father, I didn't necessarily need one. During my high school years, I hoped for the day when I could leave and be on my own.

In 1974, JV basketball started in November, right after football season ended. I was ready for a change. I had attended basketball camp the summer before and met such stars as Adrien Dantley of Notre Dame, Bobby Jones of the University of North Carolina, and Toney Byers of Wake Forest. This had really pumped me up about basketball and the coach was giving me hope that I might make the starting lineup. It turns out that I did earn a spot as a shooting guard and was a good defensive player. I scored the opening basket in both our games against

JM, but we came up a little short each game. The good news is that we won the tournament championship, a feat never accomplished before by a Chatham Central Team.

Making the varsity football team and contributing to the JV basketball championship were two things I was quite proud of. I decided to play baseball with the Goldston team, instead of with the high school. I also tried running track that spring, but I wasn't very good. This is when I first noticed my lack of breakaway speed. My best time in the 40-yard dash was slightly under five seconds, but my best time in the hundred was about twelve seconds, which easily qualified for last place. There seemed to be no event in which I could excel at in track, so I decided to stay away that sport.

Academically, I was basically showing up for class. If I felt like it, I even stayed awake. Books were not cool, so I never took them home. Mr. Burns, who is now my insurance man and financial advisor, taught algebra. He gave me a D, which I didn't really deserve. He also became Director of the Upward Bound program, a program designed to help underprivileged kids get into college. On Saturdays, the other students and I met with tutors at UNC who helped us study those subjects where we might be having problems. During the summer, there was an eight-week curriculum to help us prepare for the upcoming year. There were also social activities, an awards day, and a field trip to some interesting place. The program was a very good idea but, unfortunately, some people did not belong and were a very bad influence on those who wanted to learn. I seemed to vacillate somewhere in the middle, not wanting to appear too smart (that definitely wasn't cool!). I could see the frustration on the faces of the volunteer tutors when they weren't taken seriously. Occasionally, I'd feel guilty and put forth an effort. Sometimes, I was smarter than even I knew, but that peer pressure was a real mother.

Once, during the summer program, the teachers sent me to the health clinic because I slept all the time in class. Nothing physical was ever found, but what finally brought me around was my parents agreeing to buy me a car. Looking all the way back to middle school, not having transportation was one thing I really hated. Having a car was a positive influence and I went on to win two awards that summer: Most Improved Student and the essay contest.

I was expecting my mother to attend the ceremony, but she couldn't drive and Otis had to work. This reinforced my need for self-reliance and I began to feel more and more that I didn't need anyone but myself.

At the time my Uncle Johnny died, I was introduced to Laura, the little sister of one of Jeanette's close friends. A few of us were kidding around other under the carport after the funeral and it started to rain. Talking with her and one of her friends helped to ease my sadness. I had known who she was as a child, but she was no longer a child and I fell for her instantly. She liked me as well. I was a fresh sixteen and she was going on fourteen, although she could have easily passed for seventeen.

Laura was a really beautiful girl. Although this fantasy stuff was starting to get old, it started out differently this time. We may as well have been in different states, being that we were in different towns and different schools, and I was not to get a driver's license for a while. Nevertheless, I used my connections with my cousins and a childhood friend to see Laura at her house a couple of times. I don't think her father was too pleased, but he never confronted me. I was so far out in La-La Land that I probably wouldn't have noticed him anyway.

This was my first semi-official date. There wasn't a lot of privacy. Laura really liked music, so we listened to records. At that time, the red hot performers were Minnie Ripperton, Labelle, Chaka Khan, Eddie Kendricks, The Tavares, the Dramatics featuring Ron Banks and, of course, the Ohio Players with (awh!) Sugar Foot. If nothing else, I did get to sit beside Laura on the sofa. I felt so wonderful that night, there was nothing else in the world that mattered. When it was time to leave, Laura walked with me to the car and my heart went into overdrive. Jimmy, driving his souped-up red and black Dodge Scamp, gave us a minute to say good-night. Laura was such a sweet and pretty girl. We found our way to face each other and, allowing Nature to take its course, we kissed. I don't remember ever experiencing such euphoria. The earth did shake and time stood still for about five seconds. Fortunately, I had learned to kiss from a few of my female admirers in Goldston, who had volunteered their services without my request. So I did pretty well with the girl who was most important to me at the time. I was *totally sprung*, as the urban vernacular puts it. Finally, fantasy and reality came together and it was even greater than I could have ever imagined.

I would soon learn that such an event is usually fleeting and extremely hard to recapture.

In the early spring, I was feeling on top of the world. I had two seasons of promising football ahead, we had just won the JV title, and I was in love with what I felt was the prettiest and sweetest girl on earth. Life was sure getting better! Laura and I couldn't see each other very often, but we wrote some beautiful love letters to each other. Hers weren't quite as enthusiastic as mine: for her, our meeting was not the single most important event of the decade, as it clearly was for me. I know that she wished I were more talkative; I don't think she had much other criticism.

Summer approached and I was to spend eight weeks on the Chapel Hill campus, in the Upward Bound program. I was chosen to play left field in a few games with the Goldston White Sox. We were playing the Siler City Giants one Saturday afternoon and, as I stood in the outfield, and to my surprise, I heard the fan club of my old nemesis, Eric, taunting me with *Laura E. don't like you, she likes Eric!* I could not believe it and thought, Not again! Can't this guy find his own girls? I don't remember much about the game, but I can tell you that when these two teams played, we rarely finished the game without a fight breaking out. Usually, it was because of what we felt was biased officiating.

Anyway, Laura reassured me that we were still tight and I went off to Upward Bound on the UNC campus. Soon the letters and phone calls stopped coming and the magic I had shared with Laura faded away. I would not hear from her again until the end of high school.

CHAPTER 8

I Am Somebody

By Any Means Necessary

August rolled around, football practice began, and it was exciting. Due to the heat, we practiced at night and early morning. I hung out with my friend Melvin most of the time, who sometimes liked to have a couple of screwdrivers and a joint before a game. I abstained because I needed to be as sharp as possible. I was the running back, carrying in the coach's plays for the quarterback. There were two senior backs with whom to share running duties and I also played tailback and wingback. Wingback was an excellent position for running a reverse play, which was one of our secret weapons.

In our season opener, I rushed for ninety-two yards with about twelve carries. It was awesome, seeing my name and pictures in the local newspaper. I learned later that the Jordan Matthews players were worried about me, particularly after seeing my films. I'm sure they wondered why this talent was never recognized when I was there. Actually, I would never have believed I was the one running the ball, if I didn't know better. It's amazing what being chased by a rooster can instill in a person. There were some plays where I shook off five or six tacklers with unbelievable quickness and grace. My teammates sometimes gasped during the films that were rerun before practice. I think it actually bred resentment among some of the players.

The JM game was postponed due to severe thundershowers and was rescheduled for a Monday, instead of the normal Friday. When evening Monday arrived, we went to the JM campus eager for a win. Unfortunately, they had too much manpower and beat us soundly. Many of our guys, especially on the offensive line, seemed to panic because they had never experienced being hit so hard by the bigger and stronger Jets. After seeing the terror on some of my teammates' faces, I knew I was in for a long night We could barely move the ball on offense. One time the coach sent in a play that called for me to run the ball straight between the right guard and tackle. It was a T 44 dive, meaning it started from the T formation, where I would run straight ahead from the right halfback position and then take the handoff, with no special blocking or anything. It was just the straightest, simplest running play in the book. But why was the coach calling this play now? I was going to get killed. No other plays had worked, so how could force against force be successful? The cadence was called and the ball was snapped. I received the handoff, then lowered my head and shut my eyes, waiting to be torn to pieces. The usual sound of male grunting and plastic colliding against plastic was heard all around as I approached the line of scrimmage. To my surprise, no one laid a hand on me, as I surged ahead, until I made contact with the free safety. I had gained about twelve yards, but was upset to think about what might have happened, had I been looking where I was going. That bothered me for the longest time.

I had one other chance to score in the fourth quarter. It was a screen pass with 4th and goal from the 20-yard line, following a couple of failed plays and a penalty. I caught the ball and headed for the right corner of the end zone. Just before reaching the 5-yard line, I was met by the entire right side of their defense. As I was knocked head over heels, I felt as though a team of mad bulls had wiped me out.

The game was quite a disappointment for us, since we stood the greatest chance of any Central Team, in recent history, of upsetting JM. Now we had to wait until next year. We ended the season at 6-4, which was great for us, since the

Bears did not have a tradition of winning football games. One team before us had gone 5-5, but the .500 mark had never been broken until this season.

For me, the bittersweet highlight of that year was the touchdown I scored against our other county rival, the Northwood Chargers. It was almost identical to the game at North Moore the previous year, in that we trailed 7-0 through most of the game, until I was able to score on a right side sweep and make it 7-6. The choice again was to go for the tie, or try a 2-point conversion for the win. Again, Coach Scott chose to gamble and go for the win. The extra point team had practiced a trick 2-point play that had been made popular by the East Carolina University football team. Well, our team wasn't exactly the ECU Pirates and the play ended up being botched, causing us to lose the game. It would have been nice to have been 7-3 that year, or even 6-3-1, for that matter. It just wasn't in the cards.

As far as I know, that game was the only football game that my father attended. Someone at the barbershop must have talked him into coming. During the game, the name *Lineberry* was announced several times over the P.A. system when I was involved in an important play, so perhaps he was proud . I don't remember ever talking to him about the game, nor do I remember him being there.

Basketball season came and again there was a chance to make history, given the unusual amount of talent. Only two of our former JV Championship players were being considered for starting positions. There were at least a half-dozen senior players who were seasoned and capable. That translated into a lot of riding the pine, which actually wasn't that bad, given the chance that we might be contenders for the conference title. I don't think there was another team in the conference with the depth of the 1975-76 Chatham Central Bears. If anything, we had too much talent, making it hard for Coach Craven to know who to play when and where. Of course, everybody was eager to play.

The season started as we expected, with victories in the

first several games. When conference play took off, we had trouble with about three teams. One of them was—you guessed it—Jordan Matthews. Disappointingly, we finished pretty far down in the conference standings, but got a good seed in the tournament, where chances were good of winning the first couple of games. Our guys did an impressive job and we were headed for the semi-finals...until a senior point guard (who shall remain nameless) made a foolish play and gave the game away. Everyone was really pissed off and it became a season of missed opportunities. Coach Craven took the blame.

(That particular point guard had a longstanding reputation as a bully. Two years later, at age twenty, he was suspiciously hit by a car and killed.) This was the year I met a senior named Shirley. She was bright and we had many classes together. Shirley was short and shapely, with a very sweet voice. She had an older boyfriend, who was out of school, but she never talked about him and I never asked. Shirley looked a lot like Laura, which may have explained some of the attraction. Our relationship was strictly platonic; I wouldn't have known how to make it any other way. In those days, teenagers didn't have the kind of sexual knowledge that bombards today's teens, so we had a little puppy love thing going on. There were other girls I could have acquainted myself with, but I was strictly a one-woman man. Unfortunately, I was allowing myself to slip back into that fantasy world and I became quite infatuated with Shirley. I think she saw us as very good friends and was able to restrain any deeper emotion because of her prior commitment.

Spring rolled around and again I felt sick with being in love. There were many days when I felt like I was floating on a cloud. I was sick...and sickening.

For some reason, I signed up for geometry. I never did any work and, not surprisingly, failed the class. Even with my academic slackness, that was the only course I ever failed. I asked Shirley to go to the Prom with me and she accepted. Little did I know that she was just kidding and I later became extremely embarrassed, suffering a major narcissistic injury when I found out that she was actually going with her boyfriend.

It took me a while to recover from that one, feeling so confused and disappointed. I didn't attend the prom that year.

The previous year, I had reserved the front page of my yearbook for Laura's inscription, and she did a beautiful job of filling it with sweet remarks, even though our little thing barely made it to summer. This spring, however, I kept the yearbook in my locker most of the time, despite the fact that there were several other young ladies interested in autographing it. I was too hurt to take any of them seriously. At the last minute, I stopped pouting and asked Shirley to sign it. In a few short weeks, she would graduate and be gone. She had bought me a beautiful necklace with a cameo-like pendant, which I always wore. I reached a point where I didn't know how to interact with her and usually just avoided her. I thought I had really been in love. I cried when school ended.

While I was in Upward Bound at Chapel Hill that summer, Shirley wrote me perfume laced letters, which made all of the guys jealous. We stayed in touch by writing, until things started to fade again. I began directing all of my energy and attention to the upcoming football season, by lifting weights and running during my free time. I had decided that I was going to excel during the upcoming and final season, wanting to demonstrate that I could win a football scholarship to college. I kept this to myself, but I believed that I was destined to do just that. Football had been so good to me and I couldn't imagine my life without it. Football was my friend and my savior, having helped to make me feel worthwhile and good about myself. I felt I owed it to football not to let it down.

That's how I had saw myself: Kenny Lineberry, Chatham Central High School Football Star.

CHAPTER 9

All Good Things Must Come to an End

I n 1976, I felt as though I had the world in my hands, at least for a while. Background music was provided by Earth, Wind, and Fire, Stevie Wonder, The Brothers Johnson, Hall and Oates, 10 cc, and The Commodores with *Easy*. I had become quite popular with the young ladies and wore my Jackson 5 afro with pride, along with my bell-bottoms, polyester print shirt, and platform shoes. Sportswear also included red or white Chuck Taylor sneakers and muscle shirts, which displayed my customized physique, featuring my long-since-departed six-pack. Many of the guys envied me. So much so, in fact, that I once heard, *"Man, you're a damn fool. If I was you, I'd have all these fine women."* I paid the comment little attention. At the time, I cared more about football than girls. After my mediocre football performance of the previous year, I was getting ready for the grand finale. I planned to shock the world so the college scouts would beat the door down to get me. I acknowledge that I may have used this grandiose thinking as a coping mechanism! I set my rushing goal at 1000 yards and truly believed I could do it. I had to. The only thing I felt that I was really good at was sports and I had just started to get used to the perks that came along with being a winner.

August rolled around and photo day arrived. Features were done on the three county teams, with the focus on expectations, strengths, and weaknesses. Central was picked to be a potential contender in the Central Tar Heel 2A Conference for the first times since integration. I was proud to be a part of that team and was one of four or five black players on the roster. Three of us were starters. There was Warren, the fullback, who was built like a bowling ball and solid as a rock. Henry, our left tackle, didn't talk a lot but usually got the job done. I was the tailback, known for quickness and my ability to catch the ball. Whereas Warren was big enough and strong enough to take on the average defender, I depended on the offensive line for protection. I was glad to have him block for me on those power plays where I got the football. Practice was serious business that season because we wanted to live up to our potential. Offensively, we felt our players were as good as any in the conference. We had All Conference Players at wide receiver, defensive end, and quarterback. My aspiration was to have an all-conference season for myself. I had to do it, no exceptions. After all, I had come a long way from 7th Grade to playing on one of the best teams in the area...and as the top running back. I had made a name for myself and I intended to leave Central with a bang.

Over the summer, for some reason, Otis felt it was time for my name to be Headen, so he took it upon himself to make the change through the school's office. My feelings were mixed about that. I thought it was good that he wanted to acknowledge me as his son, but why now? I had made the Lineberry name well known and many of my peers seemed to have fun with the name, using several different pronunciations (usually "Lineburr"). Coach Scott called me aside and asked me which name I preferred. For almost eighteen years it had been Lineberry; I didn't see any way I could change it that suddenly, so I told him I wished to continue to be Lineberry, that now wasn't a good time or place to undertake such a drastic change. So I really had two names throughout that senior year: On the field I was known as Lineberry; in class my teachers called me Headen. It took a while to get used to saying Headen. My sisters were upset that it had been changed at all.

The season opener was a home game against the private school, Edgewood High. I rushed for seventy-six yards and we won by a comfortable margin. The newspaper ran a photo of me running with the ball.

The second game was against Southwest Randolph, a team we usually beat. We won the game fairly easily, but I had a very unproductive night. I even fumbled the ball once, which was so uncharacteristic of me. Maybe I was trying too hard, or perhaps certain teammates weren't trying hard enough for me. If I looked too good, then all the attention would go to me.

Photographers seemed to like putting pictures of me running the ball in the Chatham News. At the time, I didn't think of the possibility of certain players maybe slacking off a little while I ran the ball. Retrospectively, I know the mentality at that time was that no nigger should outshine a white, unless that was the only way the game could be won. We did have ways to win games, other than depending solely on me to run the ball, and this diminished my value as a player.

My main interest was in the next game, when JM would come to Central. This would be my last chance to beat those guys, who I knew would be talking much shit if they beat us. Some of them even took us for granted. Well, we were going to show them something this year! I felt a burning desire to win that game and there was nothing I wouldn't do to see that happen.

We began preparing for the game on Monday. By the plays we were practicing, I could tell that I would be carrying the ball a lot. I had lived for this game and I'm sure I dreamed about a victory. Everyone was fired up at the next practice, with the defense hitting hard. We could not win this game without a good defensive performance. During the scrimmage, the coach called for one of my favorite plays. When executed correctly, it was always a big yardage gainer. The play was I-43 counter trap, which translates to the tailback *(me)* lining up directly behind the fullback *(Warren)*, who is directly behind the quarterback *(Frank)*, in what is known as an I-formation. When the ball is snapped, the quarterback fakes the handoff to the fullback through the number four hole, which is between the right guard and tackle. This causes the defense to pursue the fullback, because he just might have the ball. It also gives the offense a certain advantage, when executed properly, because the ball is actually handed off to the tailback through the number three hole, which is between the left guard and wherever the left tackle would normally be for most plays. The key to the play's success is the right guard *(Neil, a Jordan-Matthews transfer himself)* pulling *(laterally crosses from the right side of the center to the left side)* to blindside the defensive tackle, who is intentionally allowed to come across the line of scrimmage. This happens because the left offensive tackle *(Henry)* ignores him and goes for the left-sided linebacker. It's called a trap play because the defensive tackle, who thinks he has a clean shot at the tailback with the ball, gets taken out of the play unsuspectingly by the right offensive guard who, as mentioned, is pulling left. If the right guard *(Neil)* does his job and blindsides the unblocked defensive tackle *(Kent)*, who stands in the gap intended for the ball carrier, a hole is opened in the defensive line large enough to drive a Mack truck through. Simply put, Neil must remove Kent from the gap between players, where I am to carry the ball. If the right offensive guard *(Neil)* doesn't do a good job, the play will probably lose yardage, or worse.

We went into the huddle and I-43 counter trap on 2 was called. I had had some great runs with this play in the past and it just about always worked perfectly, when saved for the right opportunity. I visualized myself headed for the goal line against JM. But this wasn't JM, it was practice. Still, my adrenalin pumped: a nice run in practice helps build confidence. We took our position and Frank began the cadence: Down! Set! Hut one! Hut two! The ball was snapped and everyone began his assignment. Everyone that is, except the right offensive guard, Neil. All of a sudden, Neil forgot that he was the key blocker for this play. He didn't even think about pulling to the left and basically did nothing, since the fullback was there to block the defensive player in front of him. Meanwhile, on the left side of the ball, the defensive tackle (Kent) crossed the line untouched and licked his chops: the left offensive tackle had gone for the linebacker. Guess what this means for me! It means I'm going face-to-face with a pumped-up 225-pound defensive tackle who hasn't been touched. At the time, I weighed 155 pounds. The play is timed so that no running adjustments can be made, meaning I have to take whatever this big guy has to offer, mano to mano. He pretty much put a bear hug on me, but I refused to go down. This was mistake Number Two. Before I knew it, half of the defense was getting in on the action. As I fell to the ground, my left foot became caught under 225-pound Kent, with several other players piling on top. I felt excruciating pain in my left ankle and yelled as loud as I could, but the momentum and gravity caused the heaviest part of the pile to come to rest on my ankle.

"This can't really be happening," I told myself. The emergency room doctor said there were no broken bones, but there were torn ligaments and it would be several weeks before I might be able to run again. Coach Scott expressed regret at allowing full contact in practice. As for me, I was in total denial. I was going to play in that game on Friday, even if it killed me. I put my crutches away and was at the next two practices, trying to run on the sidelines. The damn ankle was severely damaged, but I couldn't accept that. I felt as if my determination alone would make it functional again. Unsympathetic classmates joked that I was faking because I was afraid of JM. I was really upset at the thought of it all ending this way.

There would be no more chances, ever.

The big day finally arrived. I got to the dressing room early Friday evening to get my ankles taped and to put on my uniform. For most players, it was a football game of transient importance, soon to be forgotten. For me, however, it was supposed to be one of the most important events of my life, something I would remember clearly for years to come. Playing football had defined whom I was. Without it, and without playing well, I felt as if I were nothing.

I tried to warm up with the team but soon found that the pain was unbearable and that I was probably doing more damage than good. A tear welled up in my eye and Coach Scott spoke softly to me, empathizing "I know how much this game meant to you." There was some consolation in him doing that, but it still hurt to the deepest part of my heart that I wouldn't get to play in this historical and final game.

I took my uniform off, put on my green and white striped Goldston White Sox baseball cap (turned backward, of course), and headed for the field. As I got closer, I could hear the J.M. players having their pre-game pep rally, with chants of "We want bear meat!" This was intended to get the team fired up and intimidate the opponent. Were I to play, it would have only pumped me up more.

My replacement, Phillip, was a sophomore with no varsity experience. He was a very fast runner and had potential. He was of Greek descent and was a great kid. His brother had been the varsity fullback who was injured the same season that I had been moved up from JV. I suppose this was another karmic event. Phillip liked to play around, calling me his dad and other nonsense. He wasn't in much of a playful mood that night and stood by me, asking for advice on how to approach the game. At least I could be a part of the game by vicariously watching Phillip play my position. Besides, what other choices did I have?

The game was hard-fought, and if my memory is correct, we either scored first or early, but we were outscored 26-7. Whether my presence would have mattered or not, I'll never know, but I just knew that I had to salvage what I could of the remaining season. We lost the next game to Union Pines, after scoring first, mainly because our defense had a hard time helping us stay in the tough games. Our offense scored first on almost every team we played that season. After Union Pines we hosted Denton, a team we had surpassed in talent and were sure to beat. I wished I were playing because I felt like I could rush for 200 yards against them. Phillip took the glory because the coach wouldn't play me, believing it was foolish to risk further injury when we were guaranteed an easy win. It killed me to sit on the sideline and watch my dream continue to slip away.

The following week, against conference champs West Montgomery, I got to carry the ball a few times. I had a couple of nice runs for about ten yards each. We scored first and the game was close to the end, with us losing by less than a touchdown. This was against the team that rarely lost, usually winning by forty or fifty points. I wish I had been a hundred percent.

I was ready to start again against cross-county rival Northwood High the following week. We opened with an offensive explosion, with Warren and me leading the charge to the end zone and a 7-0 lead. Unfortunately, their defense played better and we couldn't hold on losing, 16-7.

At some point I actually sprained my other ankle, though not as seriously as the previous sprain. Damn! I couldn't let that stop me, and I sure wasn't going to say anything to the coach and get benched again. I played in pain the rest of the season.

We won our last three games, as predicted, but I never got completely in sync. Passing seemed to have become the favorite way to move the ball and I no longer felt I was an essential part of the team. My last high school football game was at Denton. I rushed for seventy-seven yards in the first half. Due to the tradition of letting the seniors exchange positions between offense and defense for their final game, I didn't get to carry the ball ever again. I was so frustrated by the outcome for myself, and for the season, that I almost felt like killing someone. I made several tackles with such ferociousness that nobody believed it was me. Then just like that, the season was over. We tied our previous 6 and 4 season and with a little luck, we could have actually won another game or two. All that I had left were my memories of what might have been.

The final action shot of me flying through the air sideways, over a tackler, with a vivid image of number 40, was in the Chatham News. The following week was the wrap-up article, in which the coach described me as inconsistent as a runner. Not exactly what I had hoped. I did, however, get an Honorable Mention for the All County Team.

I couldn't believe that it was over, and that it had ended the way it did. I was no longer Kenny Lineberry, Football Star, but Kenny Lineberry Headen, the Injured, Inconsistent, Insignificant, Former Football Player. I really took issue with this. There is no way that I could let things end like this, but what could I do?

Basketball practice began, but I didn't feel the same passion for basketball as I did football. I won back my starting position, basically through hustle. We had three or four guys capable of dunking the ball, so it was going to be an interesting year. I tried my best, but all I could do was occasionally touch the rim on my lay-up shots. I was five foot seven and weighed 155 pounds, and was physically in the best shape of my life. In any racing activity, I would always be sure to be in the top three, if I couldn't be first. I loved to hustle and make others try to keep up with me. At least that's how the season started off.

There were several girls expressing interest in me, at least in an indirect manner. Shirley even stopped by my house one evening, which was surprising. I wasn't very aggressive or even assertive when it came to girls. My basic experience was a few pseudo-relationship fantasies mixed with a little infatuation, and I still lacked the nerve to approach a girl I liked a lot. This usually meant that I was available to the most assertive girl. Out of all the girls around, that girl turned out to be my next-door neighbor, Gwen. We had kind of played around, kissed a little in the past, but I wasn't expecting to have a real relationship with her. She seemed to feel that she was the front-runner, that time was starting to tick away and it was in her heart to find a man to marry. For some unknown reason, she picked me, which I'm sure she later regretted. I had so much growing up to do and I was more likely to grow wings and fly than I was to get married in the foreseeable future. In fact, the thought was totally foreign and terrifying to me, and would be for years to come.

Gwen invited me over and we started seeing more of each other. One thing led to another and before I knew it I was missing many easy baskets on the court. Basketball began to seem less and less important.

When we got into the conference games, my mind was not where it needed to be. After I missed a short jumper against Northwood, the coach had had enough of my slacking off and benched me. The peanut gallery in the stands made it clear that I was not their choice, either. My friend, Chris, actually deserved to be starting, because he was hustling well and making most of his shots. He was even dunking the basketball. As for me, I just didn't feel it anymore.

Later in the season, our all-conference power forward became ill and I got to start again. I had an 18-point game and another double-figure game, but we had a very disappointing and mediocre record. Again, we were unable to beat JM. Sometimes I think we beat ourselves by just trying too hard. I remember stealing the ball from Greg Headen, which excited the crowd immensely, but instead of using the backboard for the lay-up, as in practice, I was so anxious to make the basket that I attempted the shot without the backboard and missed it. Against a team other than Jordan-Mathews High School, that shot would have been money in the bank.

Basketball season ended, and suddenly there were only a few months left in the school year. I was trying to adapt to a life without organized sports, but I knew it would be difficult. I had so much nervous energy, and I still had a very bad taste in my mouth from the football season. In essence, I had met none of my goals. There were no scouts and definitely no scholarships. I began doing research on nearby colleges that might be willing to give me a shot at trying out. Eventually I requested to have my films sent to Coach Bill Hayes at Winston-Salem State University, a well-known and historically black college that was part of the University of North Carolina system. I didn't know anything about the program, but I liked the location and school size, plus my Aunt Lessie and Uncle John lived nearby. I had spent time with them during previous summers and it seemed like a pretty cool place.

The films were sent and I wrote a personal letter expressing my interest in playing football. In the meantime, I placed that project on the back burner and started spending more time with Gwen. I also focused more on my academics, since I hoped to be going to college in the fall. I got along well with Gwen's family, which included an older brother William "The Kaiser," a younger sister, Pandora, who led the girl's basketball team to a state title the coming year, and two younger brothers, Gerald and Darren. Fred and Josephine were here parents. Fred was a deacon in the church and he loved to hunt rabbits, sing in the quartet, and coach softball. Josephine was a no-nonsense type of person most of the time, who was an excellent cook and housekeeper, even while holding down a full-time job. Gwen's family was just that, a family that functioned like a family, and I grew to love being a part of it. The only thing I didn't like was her need to express every detail of what we did with her family. I suppose I would have done the same thing, if my family had functioned that way.

My classes seemed to be more interesting that final year. They included college-prep English, with drama, civics, and band. Mr. Safrit, the band director, loved the Beatles, Chicago, and such well-known tunes as the theme from MASH. We even learned the Soul Train theme by TSOP. I was able to focus on playing my baritone horn and actually loved practicing in the afternoon for our upcoming spring concerts. Drama was always my first love and we were starting our final project of the year, "The Devil and His Devilish Daughter," a simple comedy, where I would play the role of City Slicker, encouraged by the evil one to compete to wed his beautiful but inexperienced daughter and ride off into the sunset. I received an A in drama, with the comment of "exceptional performance." In April, I attended the prom with Gwen and wore a tuxedo for the first time.

CHAPTER 10

A Case for Temporary Insanity

The Powder Keg Blows

The farewell edition of the newsletter *Bear Facts* came out. The school yearbooks came out and autographs were exchanged. Our concert was completed, followed by a tour of local middle schools and a rest home. Graduation day was approaching fast, emotions were strong, and the fragrance of spring filled the air. An important chapter of my life was about to conclude.

Exams were taken for the last time, ceremonies were held, and we all began to focus on the future. During those initial days after school ended, I felt lost and filled with emotion. In retrospect I've thought of how, during the first days in first grade, some of my classmates were experiencing severe separation anxiety, while I was rapidly developing my own unique coping mechanisms. Now, I think maybe all that anxiety had been repressed until those early days after graduating high school.

I couldn't explain the dysphoria and restlessness I was feeling at the time. For example, I felt compelled to write to Trudy from the play, and purge myself of things I felt had gone unsaid. I never heard back from her and never saw her again. I was still in the relationship with Gwen, but it didn't seem to be enough for me. And yet, sometimes Gwen seemed to be what kept me grounded to reality during this difficult transition.

My cousin, Edward, helped me get a summer job at Hickory Mountain Farms, Inc., more affectionately known as the *ham house*, which specialized in curing and processing country ham. I had never seen so many hams in my life. Most employees were black and many had been there for years. My former neighbor Jimmy's dad, known as Mr. Fitch (*short for Fitzhugh Lee*), worked there as a custodian. I had spent many hours at their home playing with Jimmy. Mr. Fitch was a kindhearted man and highly respected by all. He had always been around to give us rides to church, where he was an officer, to Boy Scout meetings, and other activities. That June, Mr. Fitch fell dead during church services. He was sorely missed and the plant closed down for his funeral.

Some of us were at the ham house to make some money for the upcoming school year. I was started off at $2.70 an hour, which came out to be about $21 a day, or about $100 a week. Needless to say, I was never going to get rich working there. I remember getting a $30 speeding ticket on my way to work. When I figured in the cost of gas and lunch money, I was out thirteen bucks just for getting up that day. Add the increase in insurance premiums and I should have taken the week off!

I am thankful for the experience of working for low wages, since it was a great motivator. It would take me years to get a $.25 raise, and my requests were usually ignored by administrative personnel. I became increasingly bitter upon repeatedly seeing white guys in the same situation start out at $3.50 or more. I could only conclude that my time was considered less valuable. I observed how Cousin Edward, who was a team leader, was impotent to help me get a raise. I grew to hate the administration, hated how people could be so inconsiderate of one's time and efforts. This is one of many experiences that led to the "kiss my ass" attitude I find myself having to sometimes suppress, even today. If that attitude were to manifest, it would be followed by a kindly "screw you" when some white person or Uncle Tom'ish black makes a derogatory or brown nose comment. Fortunately, I rarely am provoked to show this hostile side of my personality. Occasionally, it tries to resurface, so I know it's still a part of me.

Some of the younger workers were from Jordan Matthews and I had known them since first grade. My testosterone level was at an all-time high, as I'm sure was theirs, which led to constant picking and shit-talking. I had little to brag about, given my record of winning games against JM. I had to focus mainly on the future, since my situation seemed to be more promising there, with me going to college and with my aspirations of playing football. As far as bragging rights for the past, they clearly had the edge. Eric *(a different Eric than before)* and Bruce seemed to try to make my life miserable. Often, I got stuck with the scut duties, like transporting hams from the shipping box, using a meat hook, to the metal salting bin, which resembled a jacked-up rectangular wheel barrow. There, three or four guys wearing thick rubber gloves salted the hams and then passed them to the stacker, who placed them in a special wooden storage rack. It took about 15-30 seconds to do a ham; my job was to keep plenty of meat in the bin. The guys would sometimes speed up, to make me work harder, and see if they could break me down. They couldn't. I had so much nervous energy in those days that I needed ways to burn it off.

Due to pulling the hams from the box exclusively with my right hand, my body actually became visibly asymmetric, with the right side more muscular than the left. On a given day, I may have pulled over a thousand hams. I dreamed about hams at night. I grew to hate ham and would never think of eating it.

The shit-talking continued and I presented myself as being much more confident and cocky than I really was. Being considered a loser, which I was frequently reminded of, usually left me at the short end of the stick. I usually just held my feelings inside, which didn't help matters. I tried to focus on the future.

In early June, Gwen informed me that her period was about a week late. Now this is what I really needed! The back of my neck began to feel like the spring in a clock that had just been wound up. I guessed Step One was to have a pregnancy test done. We both were clueless of how or where to go. I began to wonder how being a father would affect my future. This was something I really wasn't ready for. Eventually, we made it to the clinic at the university hospital, where she was examined and tested. The test came back negative. Boy what a relief. Several days later Gwen got her period.

That summer Laura was working at the laundry with my mother. She sent word for me to contact her. I hadn't seen her in quite a while. She seemed to be interested in me again. What timing. I had mixed feelings about what to do, since I cared a lot about Gwen. It was Gwen who always took care of me and seemed to enjoy doing so. She rarely showed anger toward me.

Like any red blooded American fool, there could only be one choice: Laura was irresistible. Her presence made my heart skip beats and put butterflies in my stomach. She made my endorphins flow like a river. We made a date for Saturday night and I was to meet her at her house at eight. That Saturday, after my baseball game, I stopped by Cousin Lewis and Ethel's to change clothes and then drove my blue and white 1972 Chevy Bel Aire to Silk Hope, where Laura lived. When I saw her, I almost lost my mind. She was almost a woman now and more beautiful than ever. Any guilt I had about being there vanished instantly. We returned to her parents' living room, as we had done two years before, only this time we were alone. Laura put some 45's on the stereo and we got comfortable on the sofa, listening to such classics as Do the Hustle, Stairway to Heaven by the O'Jays, and of course Turn the Lights Down Low, Baby Come Close by the Master himself, William "Smokey" Robinson. Talk about heaven on earth! I was sho' nuff there, as we kissed passionately. This was the first real positive charge I had experienced for months. I was back on top of the world, and I wanted time to just stand still for a while. What had I done to deserve such good fortune? Maybe this was just a dream.

The dream quickly transformed into a nightmare when the telephone rang and her boyfriend, Chucky, demanded that she remove me from the premises or he would do it himself. Actually, his words weren't quite that kind. It was obvious that she and Chucky were having problems. It was no secret that Chucky and I disliked each quite a bit, going back to the days of our sports rivalry, and I'm sure he knew that Laura and I had liked each other. The choice facing me now was to stay and defend the honor of my damsel or to haul my ass back to Goldston. I thought it wouldn't look too good for me to be making a scene at the home of these good people, even though, deep down, I would have loved nothing better than to have kicked Chuckey's ass, just on general principal for screwing up our perfect evening and for the therapeutic benefit of decompressing a little. I didn't want trouble, so I kissed Laura good night and told her I would call to check on her when I got home.

I always regretted leaving that night, because she followed his instructions never to speak to me again. I tried desperately to rekindle things, but it was futile. Laura went on to have a short marriage with my good friend Chucky. So far, my post high-school life was no day at the beach. Things were so different now and my emotions were on a roller coaster. I had become irritable and frightened about the unknown future. My mother was concerned about me. One Sunday, I left church in an absolute rage and returned home, all because I had been overlooked as one of the new high school graduates.

During these times, my mother would sit me down and try to talk sense into me. The lecture would always end with *you have your whole life ahead of you,* which was a simple way of saying "Don't screw it up now, fool."

I know that my guardian angel was in heaven, shaking his head in frustration because he or she could see big danger ahead for me. I'm sure that angel had the insight to know that the intensity of my emotions could lead to self-destruction at any time. In contrast to my mother, I was unable to visualize much life ahead of me. I had yet to mourn the past. The way things were starting out, it felt as though a road of frustration lay ahead. I was scared about my future, but unaware of what exactly I was frightened. My adrenalin levels ran high every day. At work, I was subliminally reminded of my perceived failure as a football player from people like Eric and Bruce. I had no idea what would happen with football camp at Winston Salem State University *(WSSU)*.

One day at lunch, some of us visited a local bootleg house for a cold beer or two. I had little experience drinking alcohol, so I got pretty high pretty quickly before returning to the job. Little did I know, but the emotional dam I had constructed was weakened by the alcohol. My guardian angel became concerned, and rightfully so, because in essence the nuclear time bomb inside me was becoming ready for detonation. Unbeknownst to me, much danger lay ahead. At home, the angel was setting up an intervention to provide options for an off-ramp for the incidents about to occur at the ham house.

It was a wash day, which meant the curing salt compound was to be washed from the hams by a customized machine and then the hams were hung by hand in a portable wooden rack and transported to the drying room to complete the curing process. I was probably running my mouth, which was one way I dealt with my feelings of inadequacy, fear, or frustration. Of course, Bruce and Eric would choose today for horseplay. They conspired to lift me from the floor and put me under the spigot for a little shower. They didn't bother to check the water temperature, which may not have mattered, but when the hot water hit my body, my fight or flight response kicked in and the inhibition gates in my mind exploded big time. Oh shit! This was serious, because a wave of anger blanketed me and my ability to reason totally abandoned me. The guardian angel tried to get through but I couldn't hear him or anything else, except Bruce and Eric laughing at their little prank of soaking the Chatham Central loser boy. My only words were *give me twenty minutes* and I then started to undo my apron and walk out the door. Since they were considerably larger than I, my innate logic was not to retaliate at that instant. Nevertheless, I felt the monster inside growling, as if it had been awakened and was starving. What would be the price of calming this beast? The cost was temporary insanity, because I had genuinely lost it and, at that instance, I left the world of common sense and concern for the future. Yes, I had become a certifiable mad man. I had snapped! I no longer felt accountable for my behavior and I no longer cared. The theme that had invaded my mind was simply *fuck it, just fuck it all! I can't take it any more!* Something inside was yelling at me to *think Ken, think!* but I refused to listen.

I started my car and left the gravel lot, my foot heavy on the accelerator and spewing gravel everywhere. I drove to the Western Auto and requested a box of 12-gauge shotgun shells, purchased them, got back into the car and pointed it toward for Goldston, which fortunately was thirteen miles away. I suppose the angel could have directed a highway patrol officer to intercept me and arrest me for speeding and driving while drinking, but that may have lowered the learning curve. This demon really had a hold on me. Like a broken record, my mind was besieged by the thought *kill those muthafukas, kill them!* I drove the distance home in about seven minutes, completely consumed by the anger.

My mother was at home that day, just as the angel had arranged. I burst into the house without a word and she asked why I was home so early. I proceeded to the gun rack, removed my father's shot gun, and then headed for the door. My mother realized I was not playing and blocked the door, unwilling to let me forfeit my entire future. She somehow physically held me in the house. I guess it was the angel in her. Eventually, she got me to sit so she could try to talk to me. She started the *whole life ahead of you* thing again, which I wasn't ready to hear. With tears streaming down my face, I finally exclaimed, with all of the emotion inside me, "I'M TIRED OF EVERYBODY PICKING ON ME ALL THE TIME!!!"

She calmly asked if I knew why people picked on me, and then answering her own question, she stated that the reason people picked on me was that they were jealous of me.

My first thought was, *that's crazy as hell. Why would anyone be jealous of me?* I thought about it some more and it gradually began to make some sense. And then I felt a peace start to come over me, which would have been so beautiful, if I didn't have to return to the real world to live. Besides, I had my pride. If I didn't come back, they'd really think I was a punk. So I returned the gun to the rack, while reflecting on my newly developing insight. Damn! I was really screwing up, I thought.

How could I save face here? My mother returned to the kitchen and another stupid idea came to me. *I may not kill them but I will damn sure scare the shit out of them.* The anger was much less intense, but I was yet to feel any shame. I went to the secret hiding place of my father's .25 semi-automatic pistol and slipped the pistol into my pocket. I had no idea how to use it. I left the house and returned to work, where I parked close to the entrance.

Again, the angel would not let the police come and take me off to jail, tainting my future for good. As I sat in the car, William, an all conference running back for JM the previous year, came by and talked to me through the window. He was not known as a compassionate person and that was the first time a JM player had talked to me one-on-one about anything other than who was the best player or who had the best team. I began to sense that he really cared what happened to me and didn't want to see me do anything stupid. The Angel was using him.

William spoke to me in a way that wasn't degrading and actually made me smile, especially when he talked about what he was going to do to me if I accidentally hurt him. He made me feel much better. I had always admired his athletic abilities, but now I saw another side of him. Shortly afterward, I drove home feeling ashamed and embarrassed about my insane behavior. Eric called later to apologize and the next day we all joked about what had happened. I tried to apologize for my actions and explain that the beer had contributed to my overreaction. Later that day at the ballpark, Ted, who was the CEO of the company, gave me chewing out and said he would not tolerate such behavior. He appeared to be drunk himself. Out of respect, I listened and offered my apologies. Boy, I really wanted to get this thing behind me.

Even today, that whole incident humbles me, especially when I think about all the things that could have gone wrong. I realize that, with the worst case scenario, I would still be doing my life sentence, instead of writing a book about becoming a medical doctor and Psychiatrist. This fiasco served a purpose: it gave me compassion for inmates and convicts.

CHAPTER 11

Something Tells Me We're Not in Goldston Anymore, Toto

I held it together pretty well, as the rest of the summer passed. Soon it was August and the weather was in the 90's. Larry's wife, Eula, and Ruth were taking me to WSSU one morning as I wrestled with many emotions. The one hit wonder group known as The Floaters were riding high with their new release, *Float On*. The new group Heat Wave was becoming well recognized with *Always and Forever*, which went on to become a classic love ballad, and the Brothers Johnson were climbing the chart with *Strawberry Letter 23*, whatever the heck that is. I was so naïve that I thought you could just go to the registrar and sign up to start classes at anytime. The actual registration for everyone wouldn't occur for another week, but I had arrived a week early to begin my try-out for the football team.

We finally arrived at the dormitory and my new home, Brown Hall. I checked in and began to transport my belongings up to room 508. Nothing was really happening; there were several student/ballplayers hanging out in the lounge. I said goodbye to my family and started to get ready for my new life to begin. I went to my un-air conditioned room, turned on my 13-inch black and white TV set, and started to surf the four stations I could pick up. "Green Acres" an old favorite was coming on. I watched and laughed. My new roommate, Patrick, had not arrived, so it was pretty lonely in the room. I walked around and checked out some of the players, most of them big and muscular. There were a few groupies hanging around, but I was too shy to speak, even when the vibes were coming through.

The first meeting was held at the Student Union and dinner was served on the patio. I was looking hard to try to see someone close to my size, but saw only a few smaller guys here and there. I was scared, but I was also excited. I knew that I was on a mission, a mission to redeem myself from the disappointment I felt almost a year before.

It wasn't long before we got our playbooks and started getting ready for practice. The first few practices would be general conditioning, with no pads. There were to be morning and evening practice sessions.

The first practice was a bit intimidating, but exciting. It reminded me of boot camp in the army. There were eight or ten assistant coaches who rode the players hard, especially the new recruits. "You had a good home but you left it, and yo' ass is mine now!" they shouted. "Come on, you can do better than that, get those legs up! You look like a sissy! It's hard but it's fair! K. Washington, get yo' big fat ass up off the ground! Oh, it's so hard, but it's fair! It's not my fault. You had a good home but you left it!" Had I not been hurting so badly, I would have been laughing the whole warm-up session.

I really wanted to run the ball, but I learned early that this was not likely to happen, since there were over twenty-five other guys who wanted the exact same thing and they all were good, very good. Of that large group of backs, there were two future NFL prospects. AJ would eventually be drafted by the 49ers and Timmy would start for the Dallas Cowboys, following Tony Dorsett's retirement. I was really excited just to be in the presence of so much talent. It became quite obvious that my best chance of making the team would be as a defensive back. Defensive backs usually weren't recruited too aggressively, basically because almost any good athlete with decent speed and good hands could be taught to play safety or cornerback. There were about fifteen guys vying for the four spots on the starting defensive squad, which put me somewhere around the 3rd or 4th string.

Poot Washington was already an All American safety who led the CIAA Conference in interceptions, although he seemed not to really care about playing that much. He actually didn't bother to show up for the first couple of practices.

Reginald was a seasoned senior cornerback who planned to go to med school at Meharry the following year. Dennis, on the other corner, was scouted by NFL scouts as a sophomore. Cozart was also an NFL prospect and Ratliff was my idol. He was smaller than I, but had made a reputation for himself as a solid player, and was sure to be a starter one day, since he was only a sophomore. What amazed me about him was that he voluntarily walked away from football to focus on academics. At age twenty, he made that conscience decision. He was already where I wanted to be and was able to walk away without regret. That was really mature and admirable.

The next day, my muscles were so sore that I could barely move. Then I learned that Elvis Presley had just died and that just didn't feel right, a world without Elvis.

Soon we were ready for full pads and I was back in a uniform again, even if it was just a practice uniform. I couldn't believe it: here I was, among the elite!

The defense and offense ran separate drill stations, so sometimes you wouldn't know who you might get paired up against. There was one station consisting of a very basic drill, where the coach gives you the ball and you try to run over the guy in front of you, from the other line. This sounded cool to me, a chance to run the ball again. I soon began to realize that maybe being the one tackled was not such a good idea, especially since some of the guys were getting popped pretty hard. I was willing to do almost anything to make this team. As I moved up in the line to about third from the front, I saw the two guys in front of me start moving to the back of me. What's the big deal? I thought. Then I looked at the guy I would be matched up against. His name was Winfred and he was a junior defensive lineman who wanted a starting spot.

Winfred was one of those hard Negroes, the kind who looked like they had a grudge to settle with the world and did not give a fuck. You know, kinda' like Mike Tyson, or Lawrence Taylor, mixed with Bro Man from the Martin Lawrence Show. I felt a little déjà vu, but I wasn't going to let that stop me. In my mind, I narcissistically believed that I was much bigger and stronger than I actually was. Sheeeit!

"Winfred don't scare me," I thought. I fear no man! Bring it on! Coach tossed me the ball and I prepared to take it to my main man Winfred. I can see my angel just sitting back and really enjoying this, so I prepared to unleash the load of fury, rushing ahead full speed to trash Winfred. Contact was made. Winfred hit me so damn hard in my mouth that I couldn't remember when I hit the ground. I do remember some teammates helping to lift me up and tasting blood that was running from the big gash in my lip. I finally made it back on my feet and immediately put on that well-known *I ain't hurt* look. Of course, it was quite obvious that I was!

That's the day I decided to stay away from defensive linemen for good, since head-to-head meetings seemed not to turn out so well for me.

It was soon time for some good ole scrimmage practice. For my first college football practice play, I lined up at left cornerback and faced off with Billy D. *(no relation to Colt 45 Billy Dee),* a junior starting wide receiver being scouted by the Minnesota Vikings, 6' 3", 190 pounds, and ran a 4.5 second forty yard dash effortlessly. K.B. was at quarterback. K.B. would later be given a shot with the Detroit Lions and would eventually return to WSSU as Head Football Coach, where he'd serve for many years

The huddle broke and it was on. The ball was snapped and Billy headed downfield like the Roadrunner on steroids on a slant pattern. *Beep! Beep!* He zoomed past me, as if I were standing still. I turned to sprint with him, but I was no match for those long legs. I hadn't realized that the ball was already in the air, lobbed high with precision timing. My only chance for making a play was to line up with the path the ball was traveling and then leap about six feet into the air to bat it down or intercept the pass. There was only one thing wrong with that: I could only leap about two feet, since I am a human being (and not Clark Kent, as I was often referred to because of my thick-framed glasses).

I watched the ball soar over my extended arms and into the hands of Billy, who then trotted into the end zone. I had been burned badly. For a defensive back, being burned is the equivalence of death. I felt about six inches tall and my confidence took a big hit. Doubt started to grow within me and I had thoughts that I might not succeed. Maybe this is not where I really belong? *No! I just needed to try harder*, I thought, but trying harder only seemed to make things worse and I felt more and more like a total screw-up.

The start of this season was in total contrast to that of the previous year. Instead of being a football star, I felt like a rodeo clown. I didn't want to go out this way, so I got on my knees one day and had a long talk with God. I begged him not to let me be cut from the team and made the usual promises one makes to God, when in a desperate situation. The guardian angel made sure the prayer got through, even though he knew well that I had no idea for what I was even praying. I had chosen this path, which meant I had to learn all the lessons that this pathway would offer me.

I did make the team and that, in itself, supplied my ego with the proof that I had some overall worth. It also gave me a much-needed sense of belonging. I was granted full practice privileges, but would be a reserve for game situations. In essence, I had won the starting position for holding the big red dummy bags in practice, so the real players could make contact with them when running through the game plan for the upcoming games.

The season started off with a hundred and six candidates at the opening practice and was soon cut to about sixty players. There was some consolation in this thought: I held my dummy with pride! The real lesson came from accepting the humility associated with falling from the emotional high I had felt a year ago. Now, my view was from the context of the very bottom, yet I felt so grateful just to belong to a group that was valued by others.

"Those first shall be last and those last shall be first."

This symbolic fall from grace had been initiated with my ankle injury. Within this whole process there lay a metaphor for life in general. I was granted the experience to see the view from the top and the bottom and to understand, through retrospective contemplation, that *one cannot exist without the other*. Ultimately, both positions hold equal value on the blind scale of universal balance. I felt I was obligated to continue the path I was on until another fork in the road presented itself.

The college curriculum was surprisingly much easier than I had expected. I made the Dean's list the first and second semester. This year, my parents were present for Awards Day. I felt more encouraged by this. My aspirations at that time were to become a Physical Education teacher and coach (which I now find ironic since Mr. Ken Elliott from Middle School, whom I had seen as an enemy, was unconsciously one of my first role models), but I have always left myself open to opportunity. Football no longer gave me a good feeling, mainly because I began to realize that the competition level at college was light years ahead of high school. For everything that I could do well on the field, there were at least ten people who could do it better, and with half the effort. No longer could I base my self-esteem on the quality of my play, because my common sense told me that it wasn't worth the effort.

Had I continued that coping strategy, I probably would have ended up killing myself, but I had chosen this path and I wasn't a quitter. I had come this far and, somehow, I wanted to see this thing through.

I made A's on my first exams in Biology, World Civilization, and Chemistry. I had forgotten how much fun it could be to learn. I guess I began to feel that learning had more value to it at this level of higher education. The instructors, for the most part, seemed to care about how the students did. I was better shielded from peer pressure than in high school, because there were more than a few students who took learning seriously. There were also the students who did just enough to get by and those who got by any way they could. There were also those who would never get by and who would last only a short while.

Academics on the football team were a joke. If there was one place where I had an advantage over the jocks, it was in the books. When a history exam was placed in front of them, I'm sure that many felt much as I did when I was on the field.

I started to become popular as the team nerd. Guys would make fun of me, and then the next day they'd be trying to talk me into taking an exam for them. Some of the better athletes were pitiful, having been allowed to slide through high school without learning diddly squat. There was also a system in place in college that allowed this. It was really unfair to them because, after their eligibility was used up, nobody cared anything about them.

I was trying to manage my academics, plus make football practices, spend time with my new friends, and carry on a relationship back home with Gwen. During the first semester, I went home almost every weekend, getting there any way I could. Gwen still meant a lot to me and it was very difficult deciding my priorities. On one of those weekends I found out that Otis was in the hospital with a heart attack. I was scared because I thought he might not pull through. I started bargaining with God again about all the great things I was going to do if He would let him live.

Ruth and I went to the hospital to visit. She and I always seemed to have to fall into the leadership role in times of crisis. Earl wouldn't have much of anything to say to Otis through most of his adult life. He felt that Otis had betrayed him and his mother through his involvement with Ruth and me, and then there was the way events unfolded after his mother's death. He really had an issue with the matter. Unfortunately, Otis did not have a gift for fatherly communication. If he had been able to clarify and bring to closure some of the consequences of his past behaviors, it could have made a big difference for all of us. Instead, he let issues fester, so that we had to think whatever came to mind and work out things by any means available...or not at all.

Ruth was pretty much in it for the long haul and sought what happiness she could, wherever it could be found. This was usually through church or community activities, or through her grandchildren. I loved Otis, but I never told him because the channels for such sentiment had never been developed. The expression of affection was pretty much unheard of in our family. We felt for each other, just like any other family, I'm sure, but there was virtually no means to express it. I suppose a nice, quiet dysfunction is preferable to the family with the alcoholic parents who beat the hell out of each other and curse at each other.

As we drove to Lee County Hospital in Sanford, I began to reflect on how I had only a little less than four years to even know my father, and now he might actually die. We saw him in ICU. He was appearing quite sedated but comfortable, and able to recognize us. From what now I know about his fear of hospitals, I'm sure they probably had to load him up with IV valium to keep him from freaking out. By the love of God, he went on to make a full recovery and I always wondered if my prayer made any difference.

With so many changes and things happening in my life, I began to feel very tense, to the point that my neck hurt in the back. Retrospectively, I remembered a time in middle school football when I injured my neck running the ball in practice. Based on the symptoms, I had probably fractured a cervical vertebra. I never received medical attention, but it probably wouldn't have made any difference anyway, as far as treatment mattered. From that point on, whenever I became stressed, my neck ached severely.

I was starting to feel a bit overwhelmed, having to compartmentalize my life so much, just to function daily. I have always chosen to fight my own battles and solve things on my own and I never wanted to depend on anyone for anything. I did go to the student health infirmary to see Dr. M., who was probably just there to make some extra money. Dr. M said, "Son you just got tension in your neck." He wrote me a prescription for valium (5 mg) to be taken three times a day, which was just what I needed. Just what I needed, that is, to let the fool in me come forth. My neck tension went away pretty quickly, but I became extremely relaxed and disinhibited. I put on a show with my friends in the cafeteria, joking around with staff and clowning around.

Practices weren't so bad anymore, since the season had started. The team was undefeated and would eventually go on to have a perfect season in the CIAA conference and then meet South Carolina State in the Gold Bowl in Richmond, VA. As for myself, I was content with going home on the weekend and getting involved in a good pick-up game of tackle. I easily became very short of breath and my muscles were flaccid and weakened. I sometimes felt like I was actually going to die, when exerting myself. I blamed it on the pills I was taking everyday and started to re-evaluate things. I thought that, even though my neck no longer hurt, I hated the way I was feeling. I felt drained all the time and I had no energy. I was just as worried about my situation, but I wasn't feeling the tension anymore. Five milligrams of valium was not the answer I was looking for and I knew that I needed more help and guidance. So, what better place was there to go than student counseling?

I presented to the receptionist between classes one day and told her that I needed someone to talk with. I was set up to see Mr. Armstrong. I was a little upset because I had seen a youthful-appearing lady counselor come out of her office to get a client and she seemed more like my speed. As fate would have it, Mr. Armstrong invited me into his office. He was a very neat, articulate person with a thick mustache, and he loved to wear turtleneck sweaters. He had subtle, effeminate mannerisms, but I never really paid much attention to that. I just wanted some help. I began to run down my problems about football, classes, the girlfriend back home, etc. I showed him my bottle of pills, which he took from my hand. Very deliberately, he held the bottle up and released it, where it fell directly into the trashcan. "First of all," he said, "you don't need these." He proceeded to give me a brief lecture on how the chemicals build up in your body and how bad that is for you.

One good thing about old George Armstrong was he was always straight to the point, love it or leave it. In little or no time, he had surmised that I needed to break up with Gwen and start planning to become a doctor. He kept talking about how anyone could mess up sheets and there being plenty of time for romance in the future. I didn't really want to hear some of this; it was a little bit radical for me. He then went on about doctors living the good life and all the other associated benefits. Initially, I thought the brother was out of his mind. There were no medical doctors from Goldston, and if there were, he or she certainly wouldn't be black. I had never considered breaking up with Gwen and didn't really see that happening.

This meeting left me with a lot to ponder and opened my eyes to the unlimited possibilities of my dreams. At least now I was starting to realize that my destiny was in my own hands. I had heard somewhere that the most important thing is to be prepared for opportunity, because you never know when or where opportunity will present itself. And when it does, it is indeed sad for opportunity to find you unprepared.

Thinking back about Mr. Armstrong brings that pearl of wisdom to mind. It has been one principle by which I have tried to live my life. I met with him a few more times and then never saw or heard of him again. As Illyana Vanzant has so eloquently stated, "People come into your life either 1) for a reason, 2) for a season, or 3) for a lifetime." Mr. Armstrong was placed in my life for a reason, as were countless other souls who have contributed to molding me into the person I am today.

The 1977 WSSU Football Rams went undefeated and their perfect record was done without any meaningful help from me. This gave me the identity of Ken Kenneth Kenny Lineberry Headen, insignificant as a college football player but still trying to fit in somewhere. From my narcissistic perspective, I felt demeaned and defeated and was forced to look at reality. My savior and friend, football, had betrayed and forsaken me. Football acted as though it no longer recognized me. Football had moved on, leaving me behind, no longer a foundation of personal pride for me, or just maybe football was fixated and I was starting to move on. I felt at the bottom, and it was up to me to find my way out. I met with coach Hayes one last time, as a cancer patient would meet with his oncologist and asking for the straight truth. Is it reasonable to continue being part of the football team? What can I expect?

Coach Hayes, at heart, was a very good man. He was a tall, rugged looking ex-college athlete who played at NCCU when my sister was there. He had battle scars and a crooked smile. Coach Hayes usually was compassionate and really seemed to care about his players. He gave me encouragement, using Larry Ratliff as an example of the underdog emerging triumphant. He respected my intestinal fortitude and recognized the role being on the team played for me. In other words, he told me a bold-faced lie because he didn't want to take hope away from me. He did do me a favor by comparing me to Larry Ratliff, because Larry saw the real practicality that football would play in his future. He demonstrated his competence as a player, and then turned his back on football to concentrate on doing his best in academics. He knew that in football, at this level, an athlete could only be pimped for his athletic abilities. Once that was gone, so was his usefulness.

So where did this leave me? My athletic ability at its best would never consistently match any of the guys against whom I would compete for playing time, not to mention the new recruits from the upcoming year. Logically, this meant that it was time to focus my attention to areas where I might have more going for myself.

In my heart, I knew that this would entail a return to academics, where the playing field was even and I was guaranteed to get out whatever I put in. On the other hand, walking away now would be accepting defeat, unlike Ratliff, who had demonstrated his competence as a college football player before making his exit quite honorably. If I walked away now, football would have the last laugh and I would go down in the football annals as a big joke, and all that had been accomplished in high school would become null and void. In my heart and mind, this was my reality at the time. I would just have to wait for a sign.

CHAPTER 12

What Goes Around Comes Around

Ali made a movie about his life entitled "The Greatest," proving that popularity outweighs acting ability. Yet, George Benson produced a classic inspirational recording as part of the soundtrack. "The Greatest Love of All," made me wish so badly that I had just a little bit of singing talent. At the then present time, a brand new freaky artist known simply as "Prince" was planning to release his first big seller, "Soft and Wet." I finished the first semester with a 3.4 grade point average, which gave me something to feel good about. Unfortunately, that pressure not to be too good a student was ever present. It didn't seem to bother me as much, though, when the other players referred to me as Clark Kent, Mister Peabody, or White Boy. I suppose that pressure kept me somewhat rounded and not a total nerd, because I felt compelled to be a little naughty and shoot pool for money or play cards for quarters. I seemed to lose because the concept of quitting was unknown to me. I always lost my extra change shooting pool against Taylor, Hook, or Smiley. I played until the student union closed, and then started a midnight poker or tunk game, when I should have been studying or sleeping. Fortunately, not all my friends were hustlers, and with other friends like Rice, Godfather, Tony Stump, and Rod, we usually would just b.s. and carry on, or drive to the Schlitz Brewery for the tour and free round of beers. I also had friends who were purely scholars, with aspirations of becoming doctors and scientists. I usually tried to surround myself with all types of characters. I was, so to speak, a trump character in that I could fit in with most anyone.

My friend Paul was extremely bright, very honest and straightforward. He often caught hell from the rest of us. I secretly admired Paul, and later on we sometimes competed for the highest test scores. Once I scored 196 out of a possible 200 points on an organic chemistry test and felt exhilarated that my studying had rewarded me with the highest score in the class. Or so I thought. When I asked Paul how he did, with a smirk he calmly stated, "Oh, I made a 200." Today, Paul practices internal medicine in Baltimore, Maryland. I must give him credit for being a pacesetter.

As the second semester of my freshman year moved on, spring training arrived. Spring practice was much more fun than fall practice because many of the starting players and graduating players weren't there, which meant much more scrimmage time for the rest of us. It also gave me a chance to see just how good some of the players were. Often, when making a tackle on one of the running backs such as Smiley, I would be carried an extra seven or eight yards before he stopped moving forward. Running backs like Coley, who was 5'6" and weighed 145 lbs., were so quick on the sweeps that it seemed impossible to even touch them, much less make a tackle. Still, it felt great to be amongst some of the greatest college athletes in the country.

One day, during scrimmage, the perfect opportunity presented itself. K.B. was quarterbacking, Billy D. was at wide receiver, and I was playing left cornerback. The scenario was identical to the first day of contact the previous fall, when I was so badly burned and embarrassed. As the defensive huddle broke and we waited for the offensive huddle to do likewise, I knew in my mind and heart what the play was going to be: to send Billy on a slant or fly pattern, sprinting as fast as possible, and then K.B. would take two steps back after receiving the snap and then lob the ball high enough to allow Billy to run under it, without even breaking stride, and then prance into the end zone...with me running helplessly behind. I was determined not to allow this to happen and saw this as an opportunity for redemption.

As fate would dictate, this rematch would take place the last day of spring scrimmage, with everybody watching. The offense lined up and K.B. began the cadence "blue 29, blue 29, down, set, hut 1, hut 2, hut, hut." The ball was snapped and the play began to unfold exactly as I had envisioned it. I knew that there were only two things I had to focus on: not let Billy get so far behind me that I couldn't make a play; and to not take my eyes off the ball. Since I knew what the play was going to be, I turned and sprinted as hard as I could, just as Billy and those long legs started gaining ground. As suspected, I saw the ball leave K.B.'s hand like a scud missile and then level out and start its spiraling descent toward earth. I felt my adrenalin pumps kick in as I sprinted down the sideline. I felt invincible and no longer cared about the conspiracy being put into action: two professional-caliber football players who wanted to take me for granted and score an easy touchdown. I focused on that ball like the lion would on the gazelle and I willed myself to be drawn to it. For those few seconds in time, nothing else in the world mattered. The ball was perfectly thrown, so it was entirely up to me to break up the play. The ball approached its target, as everyone on the field and the sidelines waited in suspense. I began calculating where I needed to be in order to bat the ball away and cause an incomplete pass. It became obvious that it was going to be a close play and I'm sure that everyone's money was on the K.B.-Billy D. connection. At that moment, I was in a zone all my own and did not care about anything else. The ball came down and I prepared to leap for it. I knew that Billy had a six- inch height advantage and perhaps a 6-inch reach advantage, but that no longer mattered: I would not be denied. I leaped into the air, just as I had done in high school when trying to touch the rim of the basketball goal for the first time. I felt strong and confident as determination erased my fears. I know that my left hand was at least ten feet in the air as I reached for the perfectly spiraling football. Just like with the softball in the 7th grade, the ball landed perfectly onto my awaiting fingertips. Instantly, I knew that it was mine. Single-handedly, I retrieved it and tucked it under my armpit, as I simultaneously soared through the air and came down on top of Billy. I jumped up instantly, triumphantly holding the ball high in the air. The defensive unit cheered and the offense gasped in disbelief. Coach Hayes called me over for a high five. "Way to go doc," he said approvingly.

Clark Kent had finally become Superman. The feeling was pure elation. I felt redeemed, even if I never played organized football again.

When fall practice came, it was clear that there was not a significant spot for me on the squad. I was able to walk away without regrets. In that single play, I felt I had proven my worth to myself, and that I could now give myself permission to pursue other avenues that would strengthen my ego and self esteem. This was my sign, my fork in the road. I could now accept that I was not one of the best football players, but I knew that I had as much heart as any of them. Heart is one thing you can take with you, even after football days were long ended. Heart is similar to soul, in that one cannot really put a finger on it, but you either have it or you don't.

Just like soul, heart clearly exists and endures forever.

CHAPTER 13

Farewell to Football

Hello Yellow Brick Road

M y second year at WSSU began without football. My greatest challenge proved to be Algebra I and Chemistry II and I felt lost without an extra-curricular activity. During the previous spring, I had seen a Drama Guild production of Tennessee William's *Cat on a Hot Tin Roof,* which I found to be quite intriguing. I was impressed by the talent displayed by senior actor Ronnie B. and freshmen Floretta O., and my soon–to–be lifetime friend Lawrence Nelson Mebane *(Brick,)* from Jacksonville, Florida, whose whole name I will use because I know he will not sue me. Watching the performance brought back memories of my school plays.

I suppose it was fate that I signed up for Drama Guild in the fall of 1978. Our first production was a play written by the playwright Lesley Lee (if I remember her name correctly) "The First Breeze of Summer". It was about a southern grandmother *(Lucretia)* reliving her past through flashbacks, as part of a means of making peace with her present family conflict. I was cast as Lucretia's first love, Sam Greene, an ambitious young man who impregnated her and then left to strike it rich in the big city...but never found his way back to retrieve her.

I cannot describe how much fun it was to be a part of that play. I knew instantly that I had found a home and learned that I love nothing more than feeling that spotlight in my face and intimately reacting with the audience. I am sure there is no cocaine or heroin euphoria that resembles in any way the feeling brought on by hearing that approval, that laughter at your punch line. I chased that high for years to come and recall how much I loved making myself up as an older man with a thick mustache, beard, which changed my whole persona.

Sometime during that year, Richard Pryor exploded on the scene with *Which Way Is Up?* the movie of all movies at that time, as far as I was concerned. Richard was like a messiah for me, though many who were unable to see past the profanity and appreciate the genius and originality probably misunderstood him. There will never be another comic who comes close to Richard Pryor in his prime. Entertainers today, sometimes without even knowing it, incorporate much of his timing and style into their acts. As of yet, no entertainer has come close to those early *Mudbone* sketches. During that time, with any role I did, I would always develop the character by first asking myself how Richard would play this role. I speak here as if I'm now some successful actor in Hollywood, but the truth of the matter is just as Shakespeare said: "All the world's a stage, And all the men and women merely players..."

The better you are at playing the roles you find yourself cast in, the farther you make it in life and the more you enjoy the experience of life. Unfortunately, everyone's dramas cannot be filmed and commercialized for big bucks and fame. The main thing that makes movie actors great is that we, the public, see ourselves in the characters they play, and then we fantasize about being that person or being with that person. It magically makes us feel bigger than life. There is no stronger wish or desire in the human personality than to be recognized and loved by everyone. In fact, the very thing that keeps us all from gravitating to hopelessness and depression about the negativity of our human existence, and eventually blowing our brains out, is our innate drive to exchange love with others. Many of those who do become depressed do so because of searching for love where no real love exists, or failing to recognize that which has the potential for true love.

Over the next three years, and under the direction of our drama instructor, Dr. Fred A. Eady, Lawrence and I brought several characters to life on the stage at K.R. Williams Auditorium. Revived was a long list of dramas, such as, *What the Wine Sellers Buy, No Place to Be Somebody, The Amen Corner, In White America, God's Trombones, The Rainmaker, Porgy, Ceremonies in Dark Old Men, 12 Angry Men, Medea, Our Town,* and even an original work I wrote for the Career Placement Center entitled *The Influence.* This was indeed a special time in my life, both on and off stage.

Lawrence was pretty much the opposite of me, personality-wise, which seemed to be why we complimented each other so well. I was basically shy, while Lawrence said whatever came to mind. I was often reserved and Lawrence was overconfident. I sought confidence and I had no girlfriends (except Gwen), while Lawrence had many girlfriends. I tried to avoid attention, but Lawrence was always at the center of attention. From a psychological standpoint, I was the prototypical introvert, whereas Lawrence was the extroverted counterpart. Despite our differences, we had a ball during those years.

CHAPTER 14

A Powerful Word

A Lesson in Psychological Transference

We all think things that we usually do not say. What made Lawrence so special was that he was blatantly honest when it came to humor, much like Richard Pryor or Chris Rock. Any reader who happens to be of the African American persuasion is probably aware of all the nuances that sometimes make being black such fun. Historically, laughter has been a major coping mechanism. Most younger black males understand this quite well, from first-hand experience. Caucasians and Others will hopefully be enlightened by the upcoming paragraphs.

The *N-word* is probably the most paradoxically misunderstood word in the English language, and certainly the most bipolar word ever created. According to one dictionary, *nigger* means any dark-skinned person. Other dictionaries go further to say it is an ignorant, stubborn, lazy, shiftless, and trifling individual, that is derived from the root word *niggard*. Take into consideration who wrote the dictionaries.

My dictionary would give a different definition. It is clear that all races of people contain some members with a surplus of the above traits, which supports the idea that the word is not exclusive to any single race. An ancient African proverb states that it is *not what one is called, but what one answers to* that is important. The brothers somewhere along the way high-jacked the word and gave it a neutral meaning that evolved into a positive one. One must belong to "the club" to be allowed use of the word *nigga* socially or publicly. I don't know exactly who started the club, but that's just the way it is. The club is mostly black, but anyone of any race can join. It's really all about attitude and intent, not skin color. If you have to wonder whether you belong, you probably don't. When the slave master used the words "my nigger," the connotation was maximally negative and it brought a sting to the heart of any black or sympathetic white who was listening. When an OG or contemporary young African American refers to his buddy as "my nigga," it's the equivalent of saying "my loved one or my good friend." I think this is the angry black man's way of self proclaiming his freedom, by saying to the mythical white master, "I have taken ownership of your most painful, demeaning description of me and I now use it myself and I have given it my own meaning. The meaning that *I* choose to give it. Do not use my word unless I accept you as equal to me. If you choose to use the word otherwise, I will take offense."

Notice that this description speaks for the angry black male. This is the male who identifies closely with disenfranchisement, lynching, discrimination, and the loss of Kunta Kinte's foot. Some blacks have transcended the *reflex reaction* and are able to look past the thoughtless, powerless, or power-hungry angry white who reverts to using the word. This black understands that most decent white persons don't even have the word in their vocabulary, because they have no use for it. The word is essentially irrelevant or neutral in association with non-white/non-black cultures. These groups empirically could be viewed as control groups. The word will only surpass its negative meaning across the great racial divide if *all* people one day are willing to consider themselves as the *"nigga"* that means friend or loved one. It's possible.

Lawrence and I relished being a part of this experience of blackness searching for every ounce of humor it provided.

Lawrence was what was referred to as a professional ragger, which meant he love to rag, a colloquialism for *to make fun* of or *to joke about*. When we became roommates, we often woke up laughing and went to bed howling in laughter about the collection of data we were accumulating about our people and ourselves. Had standup comedy been as popular then as it is now, we both might have been millionaires long ago.

Lawrence majored in English and was a very gifted orator and storyteller. The introduction to our informal recreational project centered around his commentary about being so excited to leave Jacksonville and coming to an institution of higher learning, where he would be surrounded by intellectual African-Americans bubbling with innovation and profound insights. Instead, he was disillusioned and found the same *ignorant ass niggas* he had encountered in the streets of Jacksonville. I found his description to be hilarious. Of course, one must belong to the family to even consider getting away with expressing such a thought.

This theme led to a campaign of jokes and laughter about commonly observed behaviors among our people and ourselves, which were insanely comical to us. We took a tape recorder almost everywhere we went, in search of authentic data. We didn't want to miss the opportunity for a golden interview moment. One such moment occurred in 1979, in 508 Brown Hall, at about 10:30 p.m. one night, when Godfather was asked the hypothetical question "What would you do concerning the Iranian crisis, if you were President Jimmy Carter?" This dilemma had a simple solution that had never been considered by anyone in the government. As Godfather so eloquently put it in his unique dialect and high pitched and muffled voice, *"If I was Jimmy Carter, I'd just say `fuck it'."*

Lawrence went as far as placing a list on the wall, in the spirit of David Letterman's top 10 list. This one differed in that it was a running list, added to almost daily and containing over 100 entries. It was known affectionately as *"the nigga list"* And dorm mates would come from all over to see the latest entry. Each trait had its own corresponding number, so we could easily refer to it when we observed a humorous trait or action, referred to by Lawrence as being "**normal and typical.**" An example might be *Number 11: Never return a borrowed item* or *Number 2: Always late or Number 65: Require less sleep or Number 16: Have a famous cousin or know someone who does.* I'm sure you get the idea. For us, it was hilarious to notice how true to form the list actually was. Of course, we included ourselves as honorable subjects as well.

The African-American family is like any other family in that members talk about other members in ways that would automatically evoke a violent response, particularly if the same words were used by a non-African-American. Again, it's not about color at the root level, but more about attitude. It's possible for a member to be as white as snow. Even the hardened thug, Malcolm Little, who became legendary as Malcolm X, grew to know this, prior to his assassination by people whose characteristics I will write about shortly.

Behind closed doors, the only blacks who truly become offended and not pick up on the humor here are usually those who truly have an inferiority complex and are insecure about themselves. Or heaven forbid they are truly ignorant. Before going further, it must be made clear that the idea was *never to degrade* a race of people, or even to be taken seriously in any way. That said, let's just face the fact that we black people are naturally funny as hell, and fun to be around, most of the time. Black people are *many other great things* as well.

With the reduction in racial discrimination, black people have demonstrated to the world that we can compete and excel on every level. We live in a culture where, ironically, many whites actually wish they could become niggas because some think it's a cool thing to be. Many readers, black and white, will find most of the present topic distasteful, or may become angered or uncomfortable. This qualifies as a very good litmus test of how the world is viewed through your eyes.

This whole topic touches something deep inside of you, causing a gut reaction. The sleeping dog is awakened now. This chapter brings the topic from under the rock, where it is often hidden. The very meaning of survival in this world often translates to how one copes and adapts to a constant barrage of stressors. This proves to be self evident by simply observing the fact that professionals such as me have consumers waiting in line for help to be able to cope with what their experience of this life has been.

The very phenomenon of *transference,* first used by Freud, is a major tool in many forms of psychotherapy. The effect is due to an overlay of memories and emotions of the people one has encountered since exiting the womb. These people have contributed to the patterns of behavior associated with how one has adapted to, and perceives, the world, and what one will feel when certain stressors present, as well as what the ensuing behaviors will entail. This process takes place unconsciously.

In Americans, this topic of race is representative of the country's conscience, based on the feelings and social behaviors developed and passed down from generation to generation, since pre-Civil War times. The feelings ran so deeply that thousands of Americans were willing to lay down their lives for what they believed in strongly. This is the ultimate litmus test for practically all Americans, affecting political views. The majority of people feel something, some stronger than others. Some otherwise intelligent people would be clueless, as to what I am getting at here, because they have developed no healthy way of viewing this basic topic. There is nothing more un-American than being ignorant of basic American history. Even an inaccurate or skewed view is usually better than having no worldview at all. At least, in that case, there exists a foundation on which to build.

I mentioned the words *litmus test* because something as basic as a gut reaction to a single word, six letters on a piece of paper, sets off synapses firing rapidly in the brain of the reader and causes adrenalin to squirt from the adrenal glands into the bloodstream, racing to prepare the muscles and organs. Make sure you understand what I am saying here. Six letters, six alphabets, six strokes of a pen, six times fingers hitting a keyboard for about one second of time. More specifically, a very tiny amount of ink on a piece of paper can evoke a strong response from a perfectly otherwise rational human being. Now that is powerful!

<<<<<*NIGGER*>>>>>

What do you feel from reading the word? There are many different reactions across the board and they are due to *transference*. Collectively, it results in a transference reaction of an entire nation of people.

First, there are those who have no reaction whatsoever. These Americans are in a *perpetual state of ignorance* which, of course, can be blissful. This set of people can be very dangerous and are not unlike many German citizens of the WWII holocaust. They are irresponsible and will get you killed, so stay away from them.

Next, there are those who *react in total fear.* This set of people allows paranoia and mass hysteria to pervade their minds. They are very unstable and apt to act out inappropriately when stressed. People from this group killed Malcolm X, and probably other prominent public figures. They went as low as conspiring to kill and dispose of three civil rights workers. They also blew up four little girls in the House of God on a Sunday morning. Avoid them by all means; they are insane from out-of-control fear.

Then there is the groups of people who are *militant* minded and *easily get mad* as hell. These people, mostly non-white, or any group with a cause for which there is great sentiment, have a major fight or flight response from high adrenalin levels. Keep these people close by, because they are your most loyal soldiers. They will fight 'til the last man is standing.

The next group is comprised of the *rational people*. They may have a visceral response, but they understand why and where the response comes from. They use it as a motivating factor for their rationally thinking brains. When they choose to act, it is in a way that will evoke positive and productive action in others. People like the Rev Martin Luther King, Jr. fall into this category. This is where true leaders are born.

Similar dynamics play out on a division of people on the

opposite side. Some may refer to this side as *the radical right wing*, ranging from your good ol' boy cross-burning clansman, all the way to our Republican presidents. Govern yourselves accordingly in regards to this large section of the country. Most rationally thinking people can easily fill in the blanks here. My whole point is that race just happens to be a focal point or hot spot where one can rarely resist easily expressing his deepest emotion. Something as simple as reading or hearing the word *nigger* can trigger a profound and genuine transference response.

There is one last group to mention here and that is the group that actually "gets it." That is, gets how absurd the whole thing is. This group makes fun of and laughs at the whole pathetic situation. Again, laughter is one of the healthiest ways of coping with stress. This group includes your comedians, entertainers, and people like Lawrence and me during the end of the 1970's era. Lenny Bruce, a Jewish comic, tried to go there but failed to have the crossover impact of a Richard Pryor, Redd Fox, George Carlin, Dave Chappelle, or Chris Rock.

As a psychiatrist, I now understand the whole function of the concepts of transference and counter-transference toward other people, to objects, to situations, and even to a *tiny bit of ink on a piece of paper.* The word *nigger* is an excellent Rorschach test. I actually belong to the left-sided rational group, in addition to the latter group of people mentioned. I challenge you to take the test for yourself.

CHAPTER 15

Who Wants to be Mr. Ram?

Experimenting With Fear

The year was 1979, the setting Winston-Salem State University. Background music: Michael Jackson and *I Want to Rock with You*.

I was becoming pretty comfortable with my new environment. I lived a dual life most of the time, going home to see Gwen on the weekends, then back on campus for my studies and dramas during the week. I was starting to get a little slack with academics and not doing much better than average work in some courses. I suppose I figured the A's I would get in drama courses would balance out things. On the other hand, Algebra with Trigonometry was giving me a fit. I found math to be very difficult and really dreaded math courses, but they were a requirement. Even today, I sometimes wake up from the nightmare of not being able to graduate because I forgot I had signed up for math class and it was time to take the final exam and I know that I'm going to fail. In reality, I actually made a 98 on my final exam, but this was after dropping the class and failing once, for my one and only blemish in college academics.

I finally realized that it required much extra effort for me to do well in something requiring precise concentration and problem solving. I was diagnosed with Attention Deficit Disorder (ADHD) at age forty-four, which probably explains why I have had such difficulty with math subjects and test taking. I'm happy that I never knew about it then or I may have started to make excuses and, eventually, lost confidence in myself. In the long run, the extra struggles I episodically encountered throughout my education helped make me a more humble and considerate person, instead of the anus I could have developed into. Readers with a psychological background were probably thinking I suffered from bipolar disorder. Close, but no cigar. I have a neurological disorder that I have somehow been quite successful at compensating for. Disadvantages have been episodes of frustration and strongly reactive moods, projection of a careless attitude, procrastination, stubbornness and wasting time daydreaming. The good news is that I finally know why I think the way that I do.

One day, during the fall of 1979, Lawrence told me that he had been asked to host The Mr. Ram Pageant, which is held annually to crown the homecoming king. It involves some modeling of different categories of clothing, a talent competition, and answering an impromptu question. The contestant with the best score, according to a panel of judges, wins the title. Since we usually did everything together, Lawrence egged me on to enter the pageant. He kept saying that I should do it just for the fun of it, and there was no one really in it but a bunch of gay guys. This didn't sound too appealing to me, but before I knew it I was at the rehearsal. For some reason, I have always tended to try different things just for the hell of it.

The first task was to work with a choreographer for the opening number, which would be performed by all ten contestants together. What had I gotten myself into? I couldn't dance my way out of a wet paper bag. I went ahead and endured the humiliation. At the time, the *Blind* was the latest dance and it required a bit of rocking and gyration of the pelvis. I looked and felt like a total idiot during the first couple of rehearsals. There were actually a few guys suspected of being a little on the sweet side and who picked it up like a walk on the beach. I don't mean to stereotype people, but certain people just seem to be more talented at certain things. That's not a prejudice, but a fact of life.

I practiced really hard away from rehearsal and finally got the steps down. The number was choreographed to Michael Jackson's *Don't Stop 'Til You Get Enough*, by Dr. Simpson, the music professor. The music would be performed by an orchestra band. I continued to think *What the hell have I gotten myself into?* I never would have thought about being in something like this, were it not for Lawrence. I think he was getting a kick out of watching me make a fool of myself. We visited the mall and I was able to talk a couple of stores into lending me clothing, in exchange for free advertisement. Now all I needed was a talent. This is where I could really shine.

I sat down for a few minutes and created a character who was a rapping wino, and this was before rap was even invented. It started out with *"I woke up this mornin' round about dawn, and got me a drink of that TJ Swann. I was dead asleep 'til I came back alive and downed me a quart of that Colt forty five..."* The monologue was probably twenty-five or thirty lines, which I had to commit it to memory, which was right down my alley. I was known to memorize an entire script within a few days. I've always had an excellent memory, at least before I started to overload my circuit with the requirements for practicing medicine.

As far as going through with the pageant thing, I was really starting to question my sanity. Why was I going through with this? Sometimes, one has to just step out on faith and not question things so much.

Show time eventually approached. I had borrowed one of my father's old suits, which fit perfectly, then found an empty Richard's Wild Irish Rose wine bottle and filled it with red punch from the cafeteria. I polished up my dance moves and I was ready for Freddie.

KR Williams Auditorium is a beautiful campus facility that has, over the years, been the stage for many famous entertainers and public officials. While a student at WSSU, I saw the likes of Rosey Greer, Toney Brown, Peabo Bryson, Ray Charles, and

Ramsey Lewis, just to name a few. The building has a balcony and houses over 2,000 people.

Anyone who is familiar with black audiences knows that when you perform, you'd better come correct or just get the hell off the stage. If your act is not received well you will be booed away or physically removed, if necessary. Black people come to be entertained, not to be understanding, and that's a fact, Jack. During the hours before show time, I was very nervous, as I normally got before a performance. Dr. Eady always told us that the nervousness just meant that you were going to do well, and he was usually right about that. The auditorium began to fill. I put on my cream-colored tux with tails and tried to relax. I knew that if things went badly, at least I'd be well dressed.

To my surprise, I saw Coach Hayes in the backstage area. This turned into one of those Zen moments, where two areas of your life meet and you realize that there is an order that your life takes, and not just an endless series of random occurrences. Several months prior, I was running and colliding with the meanest mothers on campus and now I'm preparing to go on stage with some of the most effeminate dudes on campus, and dance and model as well. I think the essence of the moment was that I was a big enough person not to let what may have been perceived by some as failure on the football field hinder my progress forward. I may not be the best at my endeavors, but I do have the courage to explore. This is the true path to success. (Off the record, those lines sound great, but the truth is, when I ran into Coach Hayes, I knew that he was thinking *Damn, Doc, this what you quit football for, to be a damn sissy?* after which he would shake his head in pity and disgust.) But what I know now is much more important than what I thought then.

That's it for the Zen part, whatever Zen really is.

The house was packed and, as the curtain drew open, the chatter was like a colossal nest of bumblebees. The lights came up, the bass guitarist began to thump, and screams were heard throughout K.R. Williams. There was no denying that there were some sharp brothers on that stage. We all had on a different color tuxedo. Even M.C. Mebane was dressed to kill.

We broke into our routine and the girls in the audience went crazy. It was like being on another planet, as the adrenalin transformed the anxiety into pure excitement. I felt like one of the Temptations. It was crystal clear why entertainers find it hard to stop entertaining: When things are clicking, the feeling is better than sex. Make that better than some sex, for accuracy.

When we broke it down, the tone seemed to almost reach a state of pandemonium. The music was drowned out by the screams and applause. I was really starting to like this and now knew why I had agreed to participate. Then a thought dawned on me: *What if I actually win?* I had never thought about that. I calmed myself with the reassurance that a non-singer had never won before. As for the modeling, it was mostly acting and while I didn't know the first thing about modeling, I was able to pull it off.

The modeling competition was probably a tie, so the talent section would be important. I knew there were a couple of remarkable singers, but most of the other talents were mediocre in rehearsals. I began to feel a little nervous again as the first few acts went on. Finally, my moment came, and I took my starting position lying on the floor at center stage, as Lawrence introduced my act as *Good Times*. The curtain opened, followed by the spotlight, and I began to speak in a style patterned after my idol, Richard Pryor. The laughs started off low and grew into a great crescendo half-way through the bit. There were a few times when I had to pause, giving the the applause a chance to subside, so my voice could be heard. I received a standing ovation. It was an awesome feeling. I no longer felt any anxiety. I knew I had represented well.

There were different camps in the audience pulling for different contestants. I had won the approval of a large portion of the audience and many were pulling for me to win. Of course, there were some haters, too. This thing was proving bigger than I had ever imagined, and it was fun.

We changed back into our formal wear and returned to the stage for the final competition: the ability to answer a question. The question would require some thought and was a chance for the contestant to impress the judges with his intellect and speaking abilities. We had answered some sample questions in rehearsal, but no one really knew what question he would be asked. I think I was probably fifth or sixth in line for answering. There were some decent answers, but nothing really remarkable, so I felt very relaxed. Lawrence was reading the questions, so this would certainly be something we would remember and laugh about in the future.

He opened the envelope and began to read. "Why is education important in the black community?" I thought for a moment, and then began to answer in a manner that would maximize my cool points. "Education is important in the black community because it is the most powerful weapon we have in today's society." The delivery, timing, attitude, everything was excellent and the crowd went absolutely berserk. Ken Headen was all up in the house, and off the hizzle for shizzle. The applause died after a while and the next word out of my mouth was *"BECAUSE."* To this day, I still wonder why I had to say that word. It was as if I said there would be class on Saturday mornings all month. Moreover, I had committed myself to finish the sentence. Remember what I said about black audiences. They love you or hate you, they are unforgiving and there is no middle ground. You know exactly where you stand. I witnessed approval change to disapproval right before my very eyes. I had been large and in charge for a while, but the reign ended with a barrage of boo's and heckles.

Actually, I was happy winning the second runner-up trophy. Michael and Curtis, the two most effeminate guys in the pageant won the 1st runner-up and Mr. Ram. They both were singers. Curtis even went on to record a record. I was pleased with the experience, but the audience never forgave me not shutting my mouth when I was ahead. In fact, I entered the Mr. Ram pageant the following year and the haters and hecklers came out full force, to make sure I would neither win nor be a runner-up. The fill-in bit I wrote for Lawrence to do between acts went over far better with the audience than did my sequel to Good Times, entitled Bad Times. Almost instantly, heckles of "that's the same shit you did last year!" ruined the mood of the moment and led to a mixed audience response. No one was aware that the monologue Lawrence did had been authored by me as well. Bad times were pretty much in order for me that night. I pretended not to be, but I was very disappointed for a while about losing. I felt I had been treated unfairly. When Lawrence and I see each other now, we still joke about The Mr. Ram Pageant. It was an experience I'll never forget.

CHAPTER 16

And Now: Deep Thoughts

Quantum Physics, I believe from the little I have learned from other authors, may hold the answers to many of the mysteries of our corner of the universe. It would be pointless and beyond the scope of this book to address quantum physics. One fact that I have learned is that it has been proven that a subatomic particle in one location knows and makes the exact same movements as an identical particle in a different location. Distance is not a factor. The relevance of this hasn't been discovered. Could it mean that a body can exist in two places at once? There have been many fascinating discoveries in the areas of quantum mechanics, relativity, and time/space continuum. The problem is that one must possess a general understanding of the basic sciences and have a strong spiritual curiosity and knowledge of basic theology to even begin to have an understanding of the significance of such discoveries. Unfortunately, when many people claim to have faith in God, they fail to understand that everything in existence is a part of God. That includes science, which is not taken seriously by many religious people who profess to believe that through God all things are possible.

People in general seem to think that religion and science are mutually exclusive. This is untrue. As part of the triad, science represents the seen or physical part of reality. Science attempts to give us a clearer understanding of how God has constructed physical reality. In essence, it gives us something to do while we're here on earth. Religion represents the unseen or spiritual part of our reality. Religion is a social form of worship that one is allowed to take home. The more people in a religion, the more simplified it must become. A religion can be no more sophisticated than its weakest members, like a chain. Religion is the best way to nurture the spiritual growth of an individual or family. Sometimes, religion encourages dependency and complacency of an individual's spiritual growth because that individual feels he has arrived just by accepting the religion. The levels of spirituality are endless, with the least common denominators being heaven, hell, good, and bad. For some, these least common denominators are appropriate. The beauty is that God has made it possible for us to develop deeper understandings without losing touch.

Mental and emotional entities making up the third point of the triad are somewhat sandwiched between the physical and spiritual, but able to communicate with both. In his book entitled "How to Know God" Dr. Chopra illustrates this and the two former paragraphs quite eloquently. The personality exists at the mental/emotional level. The personality is actually an expression of the flesh. The Bible says *the flesh is weak*. Thus, the personality is weak, which also makes it so hard for us to live up to our potential as souls from God. It is possible to reach a state where some people understand the weaknesses of their own personality and develop the ability to remove the personality from blocking the gateway to spiritual awareness. You could call these people Saints, I suppose. Jesus was the greatest ever at doing this. Author, Gary Zukav, "Seat of the Soul" beautifully expresses this idea, defined as the personality becoming aligned with the soul as a basic premise for much of his literature.

I have been blessed with many gifts, but the human side of me, due to psychological maladaptations and environmental challenges, constantly places up barriers to my spiritual connection with the Maker. The best defense against this is prayer, but like most of us, I tend not to be compelled to pray until crisis arises. By then, the negative karma has become so great that it has caused a breakdown in my ability to accept the events occurring as a necessary part of my earthly human experience. By studying authors such as Neale Donald Walsch, Gary Zukav, Ekhart Tolle, Ken Wilbur, Deepak Chopra, Stephen Hawking, and a host of other New Age philosophers and scientists, I am seeking a healthier and more effective way of perceiving my conscious existence as a triune being within the context of a brief lifetime on Planet Earth, address Milky Way Galaxy, one of infinite locations of existence for God's offspring throughout the universe.

It is essential to perceive matters on the grand scale to find a more real truth. At times, it appears that the most vulnerable of us are lured away from the spiritual side to explore the mirage of transient pleasures of the flesh. I believe that mirage has always been much more enticing than what much of today's spiritual community has to offer young people. At times, the message translates to a seeming impossibility of having a relationship with God, without reaching sainthood status. The message in general is that everything one does that is fun leads to an eternity of fire. I suppose most conclude that *since I'm going to hell anyway, I may as well have as much fun as possible while I'm here.* (At least until the next crisis or tragedy strikes)

The one thing that I think rarely evolves much is religion. I don't mean spirituality, I mean religion. The intended purpose of religion was unification of humans to acknowledge their Maker and appreciate our oneness with each other and with God. Instead, religion remains perpetually our Number One source of segregation and war of man against man. How ironic is that? At the very core lies the emotion of fear. Religion is essentially immune from critique or change because of the profound fear on which most major religions are based. Already, some readers have formulated in their minds that I have been condemned to eternal damnation for what I have just written. Anyone who truly understands God will know that this is absurd thinking. Those readers who depend on someone else's interpretation of God are likely experiencing tremendous transference to the words I have written. They may feel that I have offended God and am destined to burn in hell. I guess that time will inevitably tell.

I truly believe that most of this writing is positive and can help people, even though I might be labeled a sinner, heathen, communist, or worse by some participants of the churches, the governments, and the media—the three parent institutions of popular opinion in the United States. In our society, the once-believed flawless priests and TV evangelists make up part of the religious models, while power and money-hungry political camps feed their spin to any and all takers. "The Autobiography of P-Diddy and Snoop Dogg," subtitled "America's Successful African Americans and Role Models," will probably be a best seller, as I struggle to promote this book with my own meager monies. At least I am expressing my freedom of speech in the right way, as did Dr. King, Malcolm, Abraham Lincoln, Emmett Till, Jack and Bobby Kennedy, Medgar Evers, Chaney, Goodman, Schwerner, Rev. Jesse Jackson, Michael Dukakis, Gary Hart, and Al Gore, to list a select few that have also chosen to express unpopular views.

Most intelligent and objective thinking Americans know the plights of all these fine people. Sadly, many applaud their plights or are indifferent to them. Were it not for public support and shrewd political skills, President Clinton would have become a major casualty to character assassination during the period of his impeachment hearings. The truth unknown to or unaccepted by many is that history would have been quite different if only half the effort used at attempts to bring down this man had been used to re enforce more relevant matters, such as the agenda of Bin-Laden. I found this to be even truer after reading former Czar of Counter-terrorism Richard Clarks' book Against All Enemies. Without excusing the presidents' personal shortcomings, he effectively shows how ignorance and hatred took priority over what was best for the country. While the president spent every waking moment plotting to destroy Bin Laden, his personal enemies tried equally as hard to destroy him over an issue as meaningless as the Lewinsky scandal.

That view may be too liberal for some people, so to make it

seem less biased, let's say if *all* of the effort and resources used between 1991 through 1998 to find an impeachable offense on the President had been used to address terrorism, history *may have been* at least a little, tiny bit different. Is that not fair to say? So what, he was busted for sexual misconduct and lying to cover it up. All that tells me is that no American's private life is safe. I think its fine for people to have personal beliefs and opinions regarding morality, but I find it hard to compare lying about adultery to lying about issues that result in the deaths of thousands of innocent human beings. I suppose I could be wrong, but it just seems like common sense to me.

When will people awaken and see what really happens in the land of the free? Or does anyone really care? The average Americans are so busy working to pay their bills, taxes, and to get ahead of the game, that there is no time left for seeking the truth. The public depends on their local religious community, government officials, or mass media for processing and distributing accurate news and information. Often it appears that the intent is to keep us as ignorant as possible. Most Americans believe that these true and dear institutions have their best interests at heart and will guarantee them truth, prosperity, and a one-way ticket to heaven. There are still many figures of truth and integrity in each area, but no guarantee that what is right or true will be communicated to those in need. Televangelist Rev. Charles Stanley is an excellent example of a well-balanced man who teaches spirituality, mental, and physical well-being. What he offers is both practical and well supported in Scripture and science. He is genuine in his beliefs and does not color the truth with his own bias or judgmental commentary. Rev. Stanley is a representative of where religion, mental, emotional, and physical reality merge.

We, as a country, must start seeing people for who they really are and not how they are portrayed by the powers that be. On the course of life's personal journey, we all fall short from time to time. Sometimes we get caught, most of the time we do not. This is a simple fact of life. The important thing is where you are now, not where you were ten years ago.

A successful individual would not be where he is in the present had he remained mentally where he was in the past, since the two are mutually exclusive. This is called character growth and is a much better tool for judging a person than the status quo, which is to promote the person who can best hide his dirt from the past. I'll bet if the rules were different and the winner was the one who could document the most dirt on himself instead of on the other guy, the picture we would see would be much closer to the truth than what we see in today's mudslinging politics. The shady side of the powers that be relies highly on how information is processed and perceived by the general public. The press plays a major role here as well by deciding the priority or spin of certain information.

I'm considered successful by most standards, and throughout my personal growth journey I've made my share of stupid mistakes. I've also used bad judgment more than I should have. Had I not made those mistakes, I would not be where I am now. The mistakes, in essence, are not the real problem, but the failure to learn from or correct a mistake. That's where the true problem lies. We should thank God for our mistakes, because they provide an opportunity for personal growth and redemption, which are at the core of the real meaning of human existence on earth, beyond basic survival. I think the witch hunts of basically good people in this country must stop. If not, the moral degeneration of our country will accelerate further down its current path. Eat your heart out, Jack Handy.

CHAPTER 17

Changing Gears

Which Way is Really Up?

I began college with aspirations of being a physical education teacher and coach. By the time I became a junior, I was totally confused about what to major in. Sports were no longer the center of my universe and Hollywood wasn't in the cards life had dealt me. Academically, I felt in somewhat of a slump, since I wasn't that turned on by most of the subjects on my schedule. My motivation was starting to dwindle, which was a dangerous place for me to be. In retrospect, I now know that God always sends us what we need at the perfect time, although it's up to us to make things happen. I love the biblical parable about *the lilies of the field* and the birds. It speaks of how the lilies are fragrantly dressed in beauty and splendor, greater than King Solomon in all his glory, without having to be concerned about how it will happen. Even the birds are provided for from day to day, and never for a second do they worry about where the next meal will come from. The passage goes on to suggest that if God so perfectly provides here, then surely he will provide for his own spiritual offspring, if they just have faith and do what is expected of them.

During this period, I met a bright and perky woman in her early forties named Betty Alexander. She had motherly qualities and a gift for motivating students. At the time, she had been hired by the university to found an accredited Medical

Technology Program that would train Board-quality laboratory scientists, or medical technologists. In order for this to happen, she would have to recruit capable students from the science department. Somehow, she found her way to yours truly and suggested that the program was just what I needed. It sounded like a nice career to pursue and would not be contradictory to applying to medical school, if I became interested in doing that. The only problem was my lack of confidence in being able to complete all the requirements. Motivation just happened to be right down Betty's line.

The transference toward her was associated with some of the teachers I had in elementary school. She was good at making me feel good about myself and did not hesitate to say that I should pursue my acting. She even made me believe that I could be successful doing it as a career. In the meantime, for that to happen, I would need to have a livelihood and, according to her, being a Medical Technologist would be the perfect livelihood. She must have been a good salesperson, because I began making sure that I had the prerequisites to begin the program. It was a tough decision, because it meant I would need to spend an extra year doing clinical rotations before I could graduate. The advantage would be that I could walk right into a job, since there were always openings for certified Technologists at most hospitals. Sometimes I think I might have dropped out of college, had it not been for Betty. I was like the perfectionist who couldn't do perfect work. This set me up for bouts of frustration when things weren't going well. There have always been several things going on in my life at once, it seems, and at that time I hadn't learned to compartmentalize that very well. There were my science studies, the drama guild, my social life in Winston-Salem, and my social life back home. I wasn't willing to give up anything, so this meant I had to become good with coordinating the events of my life. I suppose some would find it amazing that Gwen stuck with me through all of the confusion in which I often found myself. Though in the end we aren't together, she has to be the most loyal person I have known.

CHAPTER 18

People Living in Glass Houses Should Throw No Stones

Approaching the ripe age of twenty-one, I was pretty clueless about how I should be living my life. It sometimes makes me shiver, looking back at that time. Through my early twenties, the work was really cut out for my Guardian Angel. Probably the wildest adventure of my life occurred during those few years while I was in college. One spring day, while visiting home, my cousin Randy came to me with what he felt was a brilliant idea, but one that could only happen with my assistance. The idea was for us to open a bid whist club. Randy was six years older than I; for a country boy he was pretty street smart, when it came to things like hustling. He was skilled and persistent as a gambler and considered himself a pool shark.

We had played on the Goldston White Sox baseball team together during the summers and I remember the squeeze bunt play that won a game against Pittsboro and brought us closer together. It was the bottom of the ninth, score tied, one out, Randy was on third, and I was coming up to bat. He called a time–out, met with me outside the batter's box, and whispered, "Take the first pitch and lay down a bunt on the next pitch. You have to put the ball in play because I'm coming home when the pitcher gets into his windup." I didn't really think about it, I just did it, and it worked perfectly. He scored the winning run easily. Later, we celebrated at my dad's barbershop.

Speaking of The Barbershop, it had been a major landmark

in Goldston's black community for many years, before I was even born. By day, it was an ordinary place of business, where respectable citizens would visit to have a haircut or shave, and would even bring their children for a haircut. Otis would sit playing checkers with Cousin Sam (pronounced Cud'n Sam) or Mr. Brower in between haircuts, sometimes with a couple of onlookers, as various characters checked in to see what was happening and then go next door for a game of pool or to gather and tell lies. Friday was the day to go by the Barbershop. Everybody who was anybody from eight to eighty stopped by there on Friday afternoon or before they went in or out for the evening. All of the news from the previous week was discussed and analyzed among the experts. There was no topic left untouched. On Friday evening, there was no need for Peter, Tom, or Dan to even bother giving their report, so all TV's were off. There was also world-class entertainment at the Shop in the form of professional signifiers, storytellers, comedians, and jacks of all trade. Whatever you needed—a beer, a shot of white lightening, a joint, or a chicken sandwich—somebody would likely have it or tell you where to get it. There was no place like the Shop on a Friday evening.

Around eight or nine o'clock, most of the characters would break up, except for the late night crew. Then it was time for five-card stud poker, one to five dollar limit, and only the house man was guaranteed to win. The game sometimes went on 'til the sun came up and one man walked away with the bounty. Most others would leave broke. A week would pass, and then all the local characters would return to the Barbershop on Friday afternoon and evening to do it all over again. There was no place like Otis Headen's Barbershop. The last place I ever saw my father really happy was there.

Randy needed me to ask Otis' permission to convert half the poolroom into our bid whist club. Otis reluctantly allowed it, but really did not know what he was in for, and had regrets later. I remember uncle D.W. commenting that if God is not in it, then it will not last. Actually, Randy and I had good intentions when we started out, but the establishment was a magnet for those with bad behavior. Within six months, the club had unarguably earned the title of *A Nigga Mess* by the larger community. I still wanted to believe it could be the classy joint we had dreamed of, but it was not meant to be.

It was fun fixing up the place, and it was a great place to go listen to music and relax with a cold beer. We had a leather covered bar, a mural on the wall, a velvet covered card table, juke box with disco lights, and shag carpeting. It was called H and T Bid Whist Club. Interestingly, a game of bid whist was never played there, in its two-year history. Lots of poker was played on the weekends, though. These games would attract every small-time wanna be hustler in the area. Fred Gray, Big Larry, Cup, Fox, Bad News, Big Reese, Bull, Kool-Aid, Red and Lois, Kaiser, Romilee, Rainmaker, Jr. Rieves and the Union Grove Boys, and a whole cast of characters who visited on a regular basis. Our biggest flaw was that our clientele liked to drink, (even more, loved to drink) so we served liquor, even though we had been denied a license. I don't think law enforcement cared one way or the other, but if a neighbor complained, the law would ride through.

One Friday night, the Sheriff's Department raided the place. They got a couple of bottles of liquor and someone had planted a couple of joints. Randy was good about taking the falls and, fortunately, I never got into any legal trouble. I think he may have had to pay a small fine or something, but business went on as usual. Most of the real money was made from the house cut of the poker games. It did feel good to walk around with a couple hundred in spending cash pocketed, when I knew that pulling a 40-hour week with overtime at The Ham House would bring in about $150.00 after taxes. I understood the mentality of a street hustler better, due to this experience. Of course, this required me to choose between being a hypocrite or an outcast with the church. At this time in my life, I saw the church and God as one and the same and took on the attitude that if God doesn't want to be a part of my life, so be it. It felt rather good to be a rebel. I have since learned that God and the church are not one and the same. Occasionally, one can find

God in the church, but the greatness of God can in no way be conceived within the concept of a simple noun.

Our own narcissism and ignorance fools us into believing the Creator only exists within the concept of human personality. God is omnipresent. We cannot perceive omnipresence through our reality, but only to a very limited degree. This is because of our status as mortal beings, completely dependent upon this earth to exist consciously. Even our human logic cannot be compared to ultimate reality. God did give us Christ who started the concept of church, but most importantly, Christ provided a way that we could relate to, and conceive of, a comparison of man to God. Before a figure like Christ, I believe this was not possible. In essence, Christ is a special education teacher attempting to help us, the mentally and spiritually challenged citizens of the universe. Without Him, most of us are much too ignorant to maintain a connection with our Creator.

Most major religions are based on the same universal truths. I am in agreement with another popular author who wrote that the biggest problem with religion is that it is not designed to ever say that it doesn't have the answer to anything. This cancels any hope of evolution with the times. The vastness of the universe guarantees that we can never know everything. We are not expected to know all the answers. The wiser a person becomes, ironically, the more that person begins to realize how much they do not know. Any man claiming to understand it all is a pure fool. Every question proposed and answered spawns multiple other questions without answers, which perpetuates the process. The church and the Bible are, at best, indirect creations of God, and came to us filtered through the minds of man, which is by no means flawless.

This whole club experience once again allowed me to take advantage of two of my strengths: my acting and my adaptability. Retrospectively, it is clear that all of this was by design and part of my field training as a future psychiatrist, since many of my patients today are comparable to some of these people that I engaged and learned about all those years ago.

I saw the evils of alcoholism to a sickening degree. Intoxication weakened psychological defenses and allowed raw emotions of despair, hopelessness, and/or anger to break through. This was where I first learned the technique of supportive therapy, though I had no idea of it being that. I remember driving Earl M, a.k.a. *Cakes and Pies*, home very late on more than one night and listening to his sobbing story about feeling worthless and never knowing who his father was. Cakes was given this name for being a fixture outside of McLaurin's Grocery Store, where almost daily he was seen snacking on a honey bun or a moon pie. Because of my own childhood, I could empathize and offer him some reassurance. In accordance with Maslov's basic human needs paradigm, he was really just searching for love, acceptance, and understanding. It didn't take an M.D. degree to figure that out. The last time I saw him, he was active in church.

On another occasion, I had to break up a fight between two men in their forties *(Bro vs. Copernicus)* that started because one criticized the other's family members. Bro was like an elder in our Goldston tribe of young people, but we were basically discouraged from openly respecting him because he was overtly and honestly an alcoholic. There were many stories of Bro being a genius and Jack-of-all-trades before the drinking took over. This is an example of an area where I think our church community seems to have failed to evolve. Instead of providing support and encouragement for people like this, most churches considered him an outcast. Bro was respected for his wisdom and candor, among us in our teens and twenties. I detested being forced in a position requiring me to choose between the Holy Sanctity of Robert's Chapel and hanging out with real people. Bro was the perfect characterization of Pryor's Mudbone and even bore an uncanny resemblance to Richard. By day, he was an ordinary, respectable gentleman, but when he was loaded, it became Showtime. *Aw shit nigga. You just a candy-ass, still wet behind the ears. You don't know nothin' 'bout no fishin'. I been where you tryin' to get. Throw your line over by that log. Grady hooked a bass over there with a mouth bigga'round as my cap. That fish was so big that it broke his line fo' we could get him out the water. Man, its some big mu'fukin' bass in this ole pond. You niggas don't know nothin'. Go 'head n use my shit, but don't tear it up. I'll go by Bobs' n get some mo' Monday. Pass me that wine, Raymond.*

Bro had apparently been hurt tremendously by a failed marriage and returned from Washington D.C. to Goldston to live with his widowed mother. He never spoke of his pain, but it was obvious. He was clearly proud of his daughters and thought of them as his prize accomplishments in life. And yet, to the contrary, he expressed his anger and hurt through referring to all women as *bitches*. In the black community, referring to another's mother or sister as a *bitch* is a sure–fire, guaranteed ass whipping of the highest potency. Since he did it repeatedly, he must have felt a need to be punished for something he had done, perhaps failing as a husband. Usually, his opponent would be just as juiced and not able to swing straight.

Bro had been friends with Copernicus since childhood, but one day at the club, a drunken Copernicus was determined to punch Bro's lights out. I spent what seemed like an hour trying to pull them apart. This was all because Bro had drunkenly made bad remarks about Copernicus' family name. Bro also did the same to Paul, and possibly several other people. He seemed to welcome the response his remarks evoked from others. Seeing the scuffle between the two men made me feel guilty about serving them alcohol and contributing to their illness. Maybe another view is that the barroom milieu provided a place to therapeutically unload their issues. The disinhibition from the alcohol loosened psychological defenses enough for the pathologically repressed anger and hostility to be ventilated, thus providing temporary psychic relief. Okay, Okay, I know you're thinking that's bullshit. If you aren't, then you should be. But that's really much the effect that traditional psychotherapy plays. Of course, it is accepted as legitimate, where as drinking and fighting is unacceptable and can result in more disease, pain, or death. Millions harbor those negative repressed emotions, and the laws of physics and of karma require them to exert force until relief becomes possible. If proper coping does not occur, the result will inevitably result in a higher incidence of substance abuse, violent or suicidal behavior, major depression, anxiety disorders, dissociative disorders, or physical conditions such as chronic pain, hypertension, infections, ulcers, heart attacks, joint diseases, gastrointestinal syndromes, chronic fatigue, insomnia, headaches, and the list goes on and on and on and on.

Getting back to reality, what were the chances of Bro, Copernicus, and Paul going to the local mental health center for weekly group therapy? Chances were close to that of the proverbial snowball in hell. What were the chances of the local church reaching out and saying *We know you brothers hurt inside, and brother we do understand, we've all been there before. We know you self-medicate with these toxic chemicals, but God still loves you just as much, and so do we. We are determined to work with you to help heal your pain and be made whole again. Whatever it requires, we will be here for you, and allow you to progress at your own pace. If you aren't ready to be saved today, we understand that, too, but please come fellowship with us today.* I suppose the odds of this happening were a little better, maybe that of an ice cube in hell, as opposed to the snowball.

The more likely response would be denial that the person even exists, since out of sight equals out of mind. The next most likely response would probably be hostility, or a judgmental command of *You are nothing but a no-good drunk, an abomination before God. Stop drinking today or you will surely burn in hell for eternity.* This is a bit melodramatic, but accurately describes the negative transference that can occur from the self righteous toward the perceived sinner.

Bro died suddenly in 1982 and was sorely missed by those who knew him.

In all fairness, the cure rate for chemical dependence is less than 30%, so the medical profession has failed miserably here as well. The two disciplines working together (professional and religious) can improve the effectiveness of treatment for chemical dependency and rehabilitation, as many programs are pioneering, but there is insufficient funding. With prudent governmental involvement, the problem can be effectively prioritized and addressed. Driving down the demand for imported cocaine and heroin is the only way for victory in the war against drugs. People everywhere are hurting and looking for emotional anesthesia. Ignoring them or judging them does not make the problem go away. These people are overloading our jails and beginning to populate our streets.

This is only the beginning. As the government bails out of responsibility for mental health treatment, we may witness an acceleration of the deterioration of our society. The Roman Empire may seem more familiar with each passing year. Greed for money and power is spiraling out of control, at the risk of our own self-destruction. We don't take care of our own any more. "What does it profit a man to gain the whole world if he loseth his soul?" Except for Michael Moore and a few others, nobody is even paying attention to what is actually taking place. I hope and pray that I am wrong, but only time will tell.

CHAPTER 19

The Very First Drive-By

One hot summer night, Gwen and I returned from a softball game to find out that Randy had been shot in the stomach by an apparent mad man whom Randy had seemingly offended in some way. This person was not associated with the club in any way and whatever he was angry about had happened somewhere else. The shooting happened in 1981, long before drive-by shootings were popular, so this guy may have been the inventor. He sent word that he was on his way and stayed true to his word. This wasn't exactly a drive-by in the technical sense, but more of a drive-in shooting. He kept the car in the road, motor running, and transmission in park. He wielded a 9-millimeter semi-automatic pistol. Fortunately, he couldn't shoot straight, having missed two people sitting outside the Barbershop, which fortunately was closed during the week. He then entered the building, shooting through the wall after seeing Randy go inside the room and close the door. There never had been a back door, so Randy was trapped like a cornered mouse. Witnesses say the determined gunman came in and fired a shot into Randy's liver, then returned to his car and drove away into the night. Emergency Medical Services came and transported him to the hospital. No one knew if he would live or die. By witnesses' accounts, all of this happened just a few minutes after I had left for the ballpark. Guardian had made sure that I left a few minutes early that night.

These events had been shocking for everyone. By the next

morning, it was pretty certain that Randy would survive. I went to work at my summer Ham House job as usual. Gwen and I visited him that evening and he looked very weak and sedated, but was in his usual good spirits. He was only concerned about the club. I went by that Thursday evening to straighten up a little. While I was outside sweeping the sidewalk, Aunt Maxine came by and a made a comment about this event being proof enough that the club should be closed for good. She may have been right, but it was never my nature to pack up and run because of something someone else did. As my nature would have it, I was more determined than ever to make sure it stayed open. My uncle D.W. once used some psychology to try to break through my dense skull. He led me to admit that I was aware of my father being displeased with the situation, especially the liquor. He then confronted me with the question, "Why are you doing it then?" That one stopped me in my tracks. Why was I so committed to a cause that, externally, I had no need for whatsoever? After pondering a while, I realized that I wasn't sure why I was doing it. I used money as an excuse, but I knew money had never been that important to me. Enough to get by was always provided, I now know, by the grace of God. Why was I so angry inside, and determined to do everything my own way? In retrospect, some of it may have been attributable to grieving the death of my grandmother, who was living with us until she became ill and was reluctantly dragged to the car by my mother and me and driven to the hospital never to be seen alive by me again. I never got to say goodbye to her, since I was in school when her leg was amputated and she eventually died.

I was really lost during that time, spiritually and emotionally. I didn't like the world the way it was and I felt it would never change, regardless of what I did. I became more of a rebel, due my challenging and oppositional personality traits, two traits that sometimes translate into the word *stupid*.

The summer passed without further event and I started clinical rotations in Medical Technology at L. Richardson Memorial Hospital in Greensboro, NC. This facility had once been the Colored hospital in Greensboro's black community.

Betty Alexander was friends with Jackie, who was the lab director there, making this resource available for clinical training. I really wasn't that turned on by medical technology training, but at that time it was the best I could do. Also, it would earn me a fairly decent living, until I knew for sure what I really wanted to do.

This year's work allowed me to develop my blood drawing skills. You could tell how good you were by the number of times you were cursed out daily by the patients. The blood must be drawn first, with stick and pain kept to a minimum, or else you would face an angry patient when you returned the next day to collect the daily lab work.

Sometimes, certain patients intimidated me. There was a time that I broke out in hives due to suppressing my anxiety. The result of the blood drawing experience was that I became an expert in phlebotomy. I was so good, I felt I could get blood from anybody's turnip. The rotations were Clinical Chemistry, Hematology, Blood Banking, Microbiology, Serology and Body Fluids. I lost my temper only once during the entire year and this was due to an unprofessional female tech who rode me every day and constantly made up names for me. When I had taken all I could stand, I responded by loudly slamming my blood-collecting tray onto the counter and leaving for a few minutes to cool off. I think she got the message, because her behavior changed for the better.

We returned to the university in late spring to tie up all the loose ends and prepare for the final exam, which would be comprehensive. Having been the pioneers for this curriculum and training, there were frustrations that sometimes left us worried, cranky, and irritable. Most of us did poorly on the exam, which sent Betty into a panic. She spoke of not allowing us to graduate, because if we couldn't pass the national board exam, the Med Tech Program at WSSU would be doomed. This brought on so much protest that Betty had to give in and let us march. I had already delayed my graduation by a year and surely did not wish to wait any longer.

Then, just like that, it was over. The feather in the hat

would of course be passing the board exam, since this is what made your degree and skills marketable. I buckled down with my studying of old tests, study guides, and textbooks. Mike and I were such competitors that I couldn't allow him to outdo me. As a backup to taking the American Society of Clinical Pathologists (ASCP) exam, I also signed up to take the exam given by an accredited certification board known as The National Certifying Agency for Clinical Laboratory Personnel (NCA). In the meantime, we were to look for jobs, knowing we would probably be overlooked without board certification. I continued part-time at L. Richardson.

Meanwhile, back at the ranch... Actually at the Bid Whist Club, a.k.a. Vegas, Randy was living in it with his unpredictable girlfriend, Carolyn. When I came home for break, he and I lived out a long-time wish of wading in Bear Creek, from bridge to bridge, fishing for a fish called Jack. We did so, catching some Jack and several nice sized bream. This was almost not to be, when I lost the stringer for a few long minutes. Out of the blue, it came floating right back up to me. This let me know that Guardian was still close by. I secured it tightly from then on. We returned to the club, tired but happy and content. It had been almost as much fun as we had imagined it would be. Carolyn was an excellent cook. We had some of the best fish I had every tasted, with celery-seasoned cole slaw and ice-cold beer.

Randy and Carolyn had a tumultuous relationship. Often she would leave overnight or for a couple of days without telling him, and he would be very angry with her upon return. The relationship was somewhere between that of today's Whitney and Bobby and Ike and Tina. One Sunday, there was a party (tea) across town at The Greasy Spoon Club. The Spoon was a rival club less popular than ours, but it did allow dancing. I never knew who developed the name for area juke joints, but there were quite a few, such as Radar's, The Shangri-La, The Ponderosa, and Pete and Shirley's. A bullet was no stranger to most of these clubs, although 99% of the partygoers were peaceful and fun loving people. It is conventional wisdom that mixing music and alcohol with a bunch of my people, in a limited space, can be like striking a match next to a stick of dynamite. As fate would have it, Randy had spent the night alone, about which he was not happy. He decided to go out for a while to loosen up some. The mistake he made was taking his pistol. Since nearly being shot to death the previous year, it was not unreasonable that he would want to have protection. This would backfire today.

Randy was at The Spoon socializing among different cliques of people and Carolyn happened to show up. Bad move, real bad move. Inevitably, he expressed his anger about her leaving him alone and one of their typical arguments ensued. There is not a more dangerous move one can make than getting into someone's domestic quarrel. Wendell, Carolyn's cousin, did not like what he was seeing and took it upon himself to rescue the damsel in distress. Why did he have to do such a thing? There was never a clear accounting of what happened then, but one thing for sure was that Wendell ended up with bullets in his chest and dead. Randy didn't have a guardian to save him that day and ended up serving twenty years in prison for what happened in the blink of an eye.

After that event, the Bid Whist Club became history. I dismantled it board by board with very mixed emotions. It would now be transformed back into the game room. The events had been unbelievable but they were true, and life had to go on.

I was contacting Central Carolina Hospital in Sanford, NC every other day to inquire if a decision had been made about the Technologist position I had applied for. The answer was always the same: "We haven't decided yet but we'll keep you posted, have a good day." When my test scores from the NCA arrived, I opened the envelope and read, "We are happy to inform you that you have fulfilled the requirements of our board and are certified as a Clinical Laboratory Scientist (CLS)."

The ASCP exam was better known and more recognized than the NCA exam, so even if I failed the exam the first time, I would remain qualified as a CLS. Betty was thrilled to death, since this meant that her program had produced at least one certified technologist. I called the hospital to inform them and was hired the next day as the second shift Tech, supervising a phlebotomist. The icing on the cake came a few days later, when my ASCP score arrived and I had passed the exam easily. I now had certification from two agencies. Later, I learned that Mike and Theresa had passed as well. This was wonderful news for everyone.

The Med Tech Program at Winston-Salem State University was there to stay, and I had been a part of it. I had not felt such jubilation in years. I would start my first real job as an MT (ASCP) CLS (NCA) in October, 1982.

CHAPTER 20

Off to see the Wonderful Wizard of Chapel Hill

Central Carolina Hospital *(CCH)* was a relatively new structure, replacing the old county facility. There were 100-150 beds, making it small-to-moderate in size, but adequate for the Sanford area. For me, it was like being at home, yet not at home. Sanford was a small, but rapidly growing, town about twelve miles south of Goldston. I started out at $7.56 an hour, an improvement from the $6.00 I was making part-time at L. Richardson Hospital, and a big jump from the $2.70 earned at the Ham House.

I found a very nice apartment for about $280 a month. It had a fireplace, a bath and a half, and an upstairs. Gwen furnished the bedroom, since she figured I'd be popping the question sometime soon. I was still terrified at the thought of marriage and kept up a wall of resistance and avoidance. We usually spent weekends together.

At the hospital, I was well liked, mainly because I was such a devoted worker. I earned all of my merit raises, plus shift differential, but had a tendency to live above my means. I was still supplementing my income from the game room at the Barbershop, until a fire damaged it. I worked a second job for a while in Southern Pines, mailing golf magazines across the country. The pay was a meager $3.00 an hour, hardly worth the gas money, but it did teach me more discipline, which didn't hurt.

I began to feel a desire to repent for some of the things

I had done in the past and had a renewed interest in religion and spirituality. I officially joined the church and was baptized. I had made a commitment, yet I knew I could probably never live up to the standards of the Baptist Church. I also joined the community theatre and made some contacts there. We did Ozzie Davis' *Purley Victorious*, and I played Officer Vanelli in *Night Watch*, and bit parts in the musical *Chicago*.

I was offered a third shift at the hospital, in charge of maintenance of the analyzers, and servicing Critical Care and the Emergency Room. It wasn't long before the challenge began to wear off and I felt the burning desire for more. Working in the hospital allowed me a closer view at what practicing medicine was like. I began observing and learning about different physicians, soon concluding that if some of these guys could do it, then so could I. I didn't act right away, but continued to learn as much as possible about how things operate in the medical world.

One Monday evening in May, 1984, I received a phone call from my mother. My 42year-old brother, Larry, had been admitted to Chatham Hospital with a stroke. Upon arrival to the hospital, I learned that it was massive and that he was comatose. Apparently, he had been withdrawing from alcohol and became hypertensive, on top of his essential hypertension, developing seizures and eventually rupturing a cerebral artery. In retrospect, I realize that I was having difficulty with shock and denial, refusing to accept that there was no chance of recovery. I could not say that he was brain dead to any family, when asked how he was doing. It was probably best that I wasn't able to tell my sisters, who were still home and had a long drive ahead of them.

They arrived on Thursday night, the same day Larry was taken off the respirator. Earlier that day, the doctor finally broke through the denial of my niece, my mother, and me. None of us could accept that he was gone. The CT scan film was convincing, even though I had never seen one before. We signed a release to have his kidneys donated and I asked the doctor lots of questions to try and feel more comfortable about what was happening. Uncle JC handled things poorly, exclaiming, "I hope y'all know what you're doing!" At the time, I wasn't sure I knew, but it wasn't like I had a lot of choices. I did remember a conversation I had with Larry the last time I talked with him, after returning from visiting Uncle Ronald, who was in the Veterans Hospital with alcohol related complications. Following a short but intense debate of a possible Jesse Jackson presidency, we had talked about whether or not President Kennedy could have been kept alive on a respirator or not. We both were able to reach an agreement on this topic, concluding that although it may have been possible, it would have been pointless to do so, given the extent of his injuries. Thinking back to this conversation gave me some assurance of what Larry would want. I honored him by not crying at his funeral. He hated crybabies.

The circumstances of my brother's death gave me the final push to apply to medical school. I didn't know what my chances were for acceptance, but I did know that it was definitely time to act. I felt in my heart that doorways were ready to open somewhere and I listened to my intuition, which told me to go for it. I began researching the application process, studying the medical schools nearby that were likely to accept me, and learning what their requirements were.

In the meantime, I had read for an extras part for the movie *Critical Condition*, starring Richard Pryor, which was being filmed in High Point, NC and New York City. The part was an ambulance driver who gets his vehicle stolen. There were only three or four lines, but maybe my break had finally arrived! On top of that, I was hoping to finally get to meet Richard. This was unbelievable. I prayed every day for these things to manifest and felt that God was with me and I wanted to accept his will.

While waiting to hear from Paramount Pictures, I started preparation for my portrayal of Walter Lee Younger in Lorraine Hansberry's *A Raisin in the Sun,* scheduled to open at The Temple Theatre in Sanford in January, 1986. If things were really starting to break, I was willing to give it everything I had.

I took the Medical College Admissions Exam (MCAT) and scored marginally, but not terribly bad for the amount of time I had studied. I was invited for interviews at East Carolina and University of NC Hospitals. As the weeks passed, there was no word from Paramount. Much later, I learned that the director had opted to film in New York, instead of High Point, and some unknown guy named Wesley Snipes had been given the part I read for. The kid must have had a better agent than me. Couldn't possibly have been talent.

I couldn't let that slow me down. My lines for *Raisin* were learned six weeks in advance. My interview with East Carolina bombed. I met with a PhD and an MD, who were honest and told me that the resources at UNC would serve me better. I also met with a young African American student who was very nice, but I'm sure the meeting was just a formality. It began to look as if I had made a mistake trying to get into a med school. Had my intuition lied to me? I began to wonder. I had one final shot the coming January, with my UNC interview. It wasn't time to lose faith, but I did start to think about backup plans, in case they weren't willing to give me an opportunity. I decided to study Sidney Poitier's acting and life, since he had given the gold standard performance for the Hansberry play back in the late 1950's. The VHS recording was almost $100, so I went to the library to check out books. I read about Poitier working as a dishwasher as his only means of income when first moving to New York and how he had withstood much heavy criticism and rejection early on, without being discouraged. He knew that, if given the right chance, the silver screen would never be the same. When I saw the hardships he had endured to reach success, I found it inspiring.

I used my tape recorder to work on my line delivery. Feeling the actual emotional intensity of Walter Lee was my goal. I had so much in common with this character that the lines and mannerisms came easily. I made every effort to give the performance of my life. Opening night eventually came and was well attended. The show ran for two weekends. There was a big spread in the Sanford Herald. Each audience was a little different, some more subdued and mature, another comprised of lots of young women who screamed as if I were the second coming of Billy Dee Williams. Often, there were times when the dialogue was delayed to give the audience response time to subside. This did wonders for my ego, but left me feeling a little embarrassed. A large group from my church attended the Sunday matinee. My sister actually came home from Baltimore for the final show. I blew kisses to the audience at the final curtain call, amidst enthusiastic applause. What a high I was feeling! I didn't want it to end and it was going to take some monumental event to equal this experience.

James, one of my co-actors, went on to have a juicy role in a major motion picture. This assures me that it wouldn't have been that grandiose or absurd to expect that it could have happened for me as well, but it didn't and Paramount never called. Nor did MGM, Touchstone, or Twelve Acres and a Mule. It just was not in the cards for me to have a professional acting career.

We ended up getting outstanding reviews and the play was praised as the best the writer had seen at The Temple Theater. Again, I started to wondered if the intuition had been some silly delusion. Maybe I had imagined the whole thing. But if that were true, the whole medical school thing was also some delusion of grandeur.

I kept the interview appointment. If the weather were any indication of how things would go, I should have stayed in bed. It was rainy and cold. I knew that selling myself would take a very strong performance and I needed all the help I could get. I felt very confident in myself, as I approached MacNider Hall in my trench coat.

My first interviewer was Dr. Cooper, a middle-aged pediatrician, balding, soft spoken, and interested. He asked the usual questions about why I wanted to be a doctor, what made me think I could handle the curriculum, and what goals had I set for the future. He commented on the letter of recommendation that Betty had written, citing me as a strong leader willing to do things that other students would not try. This he found most impressive and very likely was the swaying factor in my favorable recommendation to the admissions committee. I also highlighted my abilities and accomplishments with the medical technology job. He also seemed impressed by this. The interview went extremely well, we shook hands, and I parted with the comment of hoping to hear from the admissions committee soon. I knew that I had given it my all.

Emmett, a second year African American student, who would go on to be a successful Internist, was my second interviewer. He was very calm and confident and we had a somewhat informal and encouraging talk. I am sure that Guardian must have sent him as a sign.

CHAPTER 21

Pride Comes Before a Fall

Had a Good Home But You Left It

*I*saw you walkin' in the rain, you were holding hands and I'll never be the same.

I listened to Oran Juice Jones, the one hit wonder, croon those words as I drove up 15-501 North from my Sanford apartment to my first lecture in 103 Berryhill Hall, the basic science building for the UNC Hospitals, School of Medicine. I was moved from the wait list to being accepted as a first year medical student so abruptly that I hadn't had time to find a new place, and had just finished my last day of full-time work as a Medical Technologist a few days earlier. I wasn't sure of what to expect at medical school and I really hadn't given it much thought, because there were too many thoughts rushing through my mind. I was familiar with *They wouldn't have accepted me if they didn't think I could do the work* And found some comfort in having Mrs. Evelyn McCarthy speak with me several times on the phone over the summer. She was Director of the Medical Education Development Program (M.E.D.), designed to prepare promising undergraduates for an opportunity for a head start on the first semester of med school. I had to decline, due to feeling unable to just walk away from my third shift responsibilities at the hospital lab. I still had rent, utilities, and a car payment that weren't going anywhere, and my financial aid was uncertain. It seemed that I was a creature of habit when it came to doing things the hard way.

This was starting out to be a difficult transition. I had been away from academics for almost five years, but I wasn't too worried. Since playing the role of Walter Lee Younger the previous January, my confidence was soaring. I used that narcissism and arrogance as my buffer against the anxiety that was starting to mount. Little did I know, but that was a very big mistake.

By the time I got to Chapel Hill, it was pouring down rain; finding a parking space was next to impossible. When I finally reached the lecture hall, there were no decent seats left. Note-taking was quite ineffective. Later, I stopped by the lab upstairs, which functioned as home base, where books, microscopes, and other items were kept. Prior to the drive home, I stopped by the Caduceus Book Store to purchase texts for Anatomy, Histology, Biochemistry, Embryology, Social and Cultural Issues, and Intro to Medicine. A syllabus was provided for each class as well and contained all of the lecture material. Textbooks were intended mainly for reference. Being unaware of this was another mistake. It did not take long to find that most of my classmates were extraordinarily intelligent, many groomed since kindergarten to be doctors, by their doctor parents. Others already held PhD's or Masters Degrees in different disciplines, while others were fresh out of college and well polished in practically all the basic sciences.

I began to experience the same anxiety that I had felt back in 1977, when trying out for college football at WSSU. I felt that every one of the 159 other students were so much more intelligent and better prepared than I. I began to feel isolated and alone. The one thing I had expertise in was laboratory technology, but I found that when an opportunity to shine in this area came, I was usually ignored...as though I were invisible. Eventually, I began to withdraw and felt very angry toward the attitudes of some of my white classmates. When in lab, and there came a topic that I knew very well, and I was looked upon as not knowing what I was talking about, I would become furious within. Finally, I just said "Fuck it!"

In the midst of this frustration, I also had to find an

apartment and go through that whole moving process. Too bad I couldn't just go home in the evenings, relax and study. It would be a while before this became a possibility. It soon became evident that the semester was going to be unpleasant.

I found anatomy to be very interesting, but also stressful. Laughing and kidding seemed to be the only way I knew to cope with working with the cadaver. I was not very good at dissecting, so I was appointed the skin removal specialist. We worked in groups of four. My partners were Leigh, Roy, and Jim. Roy was an African American whose father was a small-town practitioner. We sometimes played basketball together and he was a very nice guy. Leigh was a nice young woman and Jim was the blue chip student from the University of Virginia who at times seemed to have a superiority complex. He wasn't that bad, since the most he ever did was make fun of Roy and me behind our backs, but he glowed like a beet the day his friend threatened to expose what he had been saying.

Racist attitudes were actually commonplace in medical school, but usually too subtle to be detected. It was very well known that a large number of whites did not feel most black students were qualified to go to medical school. Some didn't want blacks there period, even if some of us were the valedictorians of our classes. I couldn't afford to be affected by the attitudes and beliefs of pompous assholes. Retrospectively, it is obvious that the medical education system in general was not designed for most black students to do well. In fact, for most schools, it was not user friendly for the average minority student. The UNC Medical School was an exception, making an impressive effort to help even the playing field for disadvantaged students. It still offers tutoring, an M.E.D. program, a dedicated support staff, and a decelerated curriculum for students who, for various reasons, may not be able to squeeze the equivalent of four years of college into two years of medical school.

The tradition of making the basic science portion of med school as difficult as possible does have the advantage of guaranteeing that only the most academically elite students are placed in the top spots. Nevertheless, does making straight A's and having an IQ of 175 mean that this student will be the best doctor? The great thing about the UNC Medical School is its commitment to the state mandate of training doctors to match the population of the state.

Academic achievement is not the only criteria in choosing medical students. Other important factors are considered, such as personality, professional experience, geographical location, MCAT scores, special interests outside of medicine, and the dedication to specialize in an under-represented area of primary care medicine. Many subspecialties have a surplus of doctors, while much of the population is without adequate access to primary care doctors. It would be of little benefit to have mostly cardiothoracic surgeons, radiologists, anesthesiologists, and plastic surgeons form most of the graduating class of a medical school. If only the straight-A overachievers were admitted to med school, most would be unlikely to do Family Practice, Pediatrics, OB-Gyn, Internal Medicine, or Psychiatry. To become a doctor, a certain minimal aptitude is definitely required, but not genius qualification. The genius doesn't always have the best bedside manner, interpersonal skills, or exercise the best judgment or common sense.

Eventually, discrimination would have forced itself to end; at some point, the pendulum would start to swing the other way. Once, most doctors were white males, which could be supported because only white males were granted the highest quality undergraduate education. This guaranteed who would have the highest grades most of the time. Others need not apply. Had that policy lasted through today, we would probably be headed toward having all Asian doctors, since Asians, for whatever reason, consistently outscore whites, blacks, and all others on the Medical College Admissions Test and other examinations. Each applicant should be assessed individually for what they can add to the medical community. The University of North Carolina Medical School does a very commendable job with this. Each first year class is diverse, and assembled with the goal of meeting the needs of the citizens of North Carolina. Most other medical schools do not have this level of commitment.

An accident occurs when a number of events happen in a certain order, time, and place. An accident of major proportions was about to occur to this naïve twenty-seven year-old medical student. The first exam, covering cell biology, was a one-shot, pass or fail deal. Many students were about to see what medical school was really about. After this exam, it became quite clear that playtime was over. As designed, the majority of students passed without a problem, but the remaining students were caught off-guard. Panic could be felt in the air. Dean Strayhorn's office became like a funeral home for many students, after each set of exams. Pride, for many, was cut down like a flower in an abrupt manner. The Dean had been through this many times before.

Dean Strayhorn was a tall, lean, scholarly-appearing African American professor of Family Medicine. His mannerisms were a little on the effeminate side, but he was a straight shooter who didn't play with you. He was known to shock you with the reality of your situation, without any sugar coating, after which he would effectively provide comfort and consolation.

After that first exam, students began breaking into different cliques. Those who failed the exam, such as yours truly, sought support and comfort from one another as the grief reaction proceeded.

The stress had started to take hold. I finally found an apartment and began moving. I felt as though there was no one to talk to about the fear and disappointment I was feeling. The best Gwen could offer was to suggest I come back home and take some community college courses. She clearly didn't understand what made me tick. I would die before quitting. On top of everything, I had committed myself to work at the hospital lab in Sanford several weekends during the semester. Surely, I was having some major denial regarding the seriousness of my situation.

A retest was given, and I got over 90% of the questions correct, but it didn't feel the same as it would have, had I passed the first time around. Dean Strayhorn suggested I enter a decelerated curriculum that would allow me the opportunity to have more time to take care of my affairs and enough time to study properly and be better prepared for the barrage of exams to come. This would mean falling back a class, as the original class moved on. To me, that would have been like conceding, and this was not my style. Despite feeling overwhelmed, my dumb ass just had to do things my way. Little did I know that it was virtually impossible to catch up, once I had fallen behind.

Dean Strayhorn tried his best to get this message across, but I was not hearing it. It was similar to the Japanese in Hiroshima and Nagasaki, and President Truman.

My Guardian Angel was returning from a long vacation. He always arrived just in the nick of time. He watched me study and prepare for the big showdown in December and accompanied me to the altar at Roberts Chapel. He could see ahead to the future without any problem and he knew I was in for the shock of my life.

It wasn't a question of intellect or fund of knowledge, because I had those. It was strictly a case of preparation, and I was not prepared for final exams. The multiple choice K-type question format was totally foreign to me. I became my own worst enemy, always expecting a trick behind each question, which caused me to outsmart myself and miss several questions. The attention deficit disorder was full steam ahead, but I had no idea of its existence. I knew more than enough anatomy to pass easily, but by the time I finished reshuffling my answers I was doomed.

On the Anatomy practical exam, where there were about twenty stations, I got out of sync somehow with the rotation order, which led to panic and a total loss of concentration. I missed several easy ones, even though I knew close to every item. After the final histology exam, I sat in the lecture hall, stunned by the enormity of what had transpired during the week. I knew my performance had been unsatisfactory and I had not had a decent night's sleep in days. I felt like shit; I remained stunned for some time. Finally, not knowing where else to go, I went to my advisor's office. Dr. Norfleet, an anesthesiologist. He was busy in surgery but was very understanding and supportive. All I really wanted was something to help me get to sleep. He knew that my situation was more than he was able to handle and he had a social engagement to attend. He provided me with some cover and had me stretch out and try to unwind in his office.

I remained in shock as I prepared to mourn the loss of the remains of my pride and self worth. Never had I reached this emotional low before; never had I felt like such a failure. And all of a sudden, nothing seemed to matter any more. I didn't know what was to come, but I was sure it wouldn't be good. Dr. Norfleet arranged an emergency crisis appointment with Psychiatry. Ironically, I was assessed by a resident who sat in the same spot in which I would sit only a few years later.

Everything was foggy, but I remember him asking me several questions. "Are you having thoughts of suicide?" I wasn't actively having those thoughts, but I felt it would be nice to drop off the earth for a while. The attending physician that day was a Dr. Pope, a Freudian-appearing gentleman who smoked a pipe. He spent time talking to me about the concept of failure, using the analogy of the surgeon who accidentally cuts through an artery. "Everyone makes mistakes," he said. Testing his sincerity, I asked if he had ever failed at anything. I was surprised to hear him say *yes*. It did make me feel a little better.

At that time, I just wanted to get some sleep, I was so exhausted. Prudently, he prescribed me a single Restoril tablet, at the urging of my Guardian Angel.

These events were happening either on or around the time of my 28th birthday. I went by the pharmacy and then headed home. I don't know what I was thinking, but I picked up a couple of boxes of sleeping pills, along with my prescription. I went home but still couldn't sleep. Alone, I realized how I had blown it, and how much I didn't want to face the future. I began to unpack the pills and place them individually in an ashtray on the coffee table. I wondered if those would be enough to do the job. My Guardian Angel began communicating with me as I sat despondently on the sofa. "Ken, man what are you doing? It's not that bad."

Deep down, I didn't think I would really do it, but I felt like playing with myself as though I would, for some strange reason. I was searching in my mind for valid reasons not to act. Had I been drinking and not thinking as clearly, things might have been different. Guardian made sure there was no alcohol around.

The next day, I took a long walk up and down the railroad tracks. I again entertained the idea of suicide and concluded that this would never be an acceptable option, unless I could guarantee that my body wouldn't be found. I thought of my young nephews who had recently moved with Alfreda back home. I wanted to be a part of their growing up. I thought about Gwen, wondering if she'd be better off without me. I thought of my family. Guardian told me to not jump to conclusions, and to collect all of the data before I did anything. At this point, I didn't even know what my test scores were, and it was not in stone that I would be dismissed from medical school.

Later, Guardian sent over my neighbor, Larry, to check on me. He knocked on the door as I was cutting my hair.

Larry was a future orthopedic surgeon, a former college basketball player with whom I often caught the bus, or his wife would sometimes pick us up. I think he sensed my mood and he suggested we go check out a movie. We saw a flick with Richard Pryor and Gene Wilder. Richard was coming down with multiple sclerosis and clearly wasn't his old self. I suppose, subconsciously, I recognized the imperfections and instabilities of life in that Richard wasn't Richard anymore. I felt better after the movie.

After the movie, we went to see if the grades had been posted. They had. I chose to tell Larry of the courses I had failed. At least I was starting to acknowledge it as reality. I tried to enjoy the Christmas Holiday, but it was difficult to do so with no idea of what my fate in med school would be.

CHAPTER 22

Sink or Swim With the Sharks

Somehow, I managed to take my mind off of things for a couple of weeks. I basically hung out with friends and family. I went on campus a few times, but just the sight of the building would bring tears to my eyes. One day, I ran into a guy I had seen in lectures and we started to talk. He told me his name was Vernon and it turned out that he had the same experience academically as I. We started to become friends.

Vernon was several years younger, but we had the curriculum in common. He was from a small town in eastern North Carolina and had majored in chemistry at UNC. Vernon seemed to have lived a sheltered life and was naïve about almost everything. He needed to look up to someone, and that was me. His father had died several years before and he had a twin brother who was described as being more outgoing. Having Vernon around made me feel less isolated, and we could always talk about the classes we had in common, as well as the fears and frustrations we both faced. Vernon often related to superiors and other figures in a way that would land him in trouble. As far as academic potential, we were fairly close, but he lacked the interpersonal skills I possessed.

I was not a social butterfly, but through my life experiences I had learned how to read and react to people. I knew the need to be versatile, as far as dealing with different types of people. For instance, I learned that white people like to be right about things practically all the time, so you sometimes have to make certain sacrifices to obtain what you want. Let them be right if it can further your own cause in some way. As long as you keep your mouth closed, you have a hole card. When you are the minority, it's like being in court all the time. Anything you say, can and most definitely will be used against you. I learned to keep my mouth closed and keep them guessing.

The experience I had with the Med Tech Program in college taught me that the whole education process is basically a game and the real objective is to survive. Eventually you will learn everything you need to know if you can just survive. I wasn't the best Med Tech student, but I became an excellent technologist, mainly through on-the-job training. I knew these basic science courses worked in pretty much the same way. It was a simple matter of not being beaten by the system. I knew that the clinical years would be no problem for me. Even with the first semester problems, I felt comfortable about the future third year clinical rotations.

Later, I grew to understand that everything was by divine design, in my case. It was necessary for God to humble me in order for me to do any real good for others. The potential was there for me to be an arrogant, self-serving asshole, had things gone too smoothly for me and I probably wouldn't have even thought to give God any credit for my accomplishments. My Guardian Angel knew that God needed to let me be processed from scratch, for me to be of good to anyone other than myself. Of course, I knew nothing of any of this at the time and thought that my luck was the worst in the world.

Because of the way things played out for me, it was predestined for that I finish medical school and become much wiser and more knowledgeable. Through this first semester of med school, God had gained my full attention. I felt extreme humility and appreciation. All of the arrogance, narcissism, and pride had been killed and buried; my self-esteem was still in a coma. I started to recognize that fate hadn't arranged this path for me so that I could demonstrate how great an individual I was. When I learned that I would be able to remain in school— contingent upon never failing another course—the stage was set. This had always been when I was at my best, playing the underdog role, and my work was cut out for me. I was still feeling a lot of grief, but I knew that the monster within would not let me rest until my mission was accomplished.

I became efficient at using that rage as the internal combustion engine uses gasoline to create something useful. I was also aware of the damage that internal rage could cause for me if it was used the wrong way. There would be no more lack of preparation or surprises; I knew what was expected of me. It was not unlike the day I decided to challenge the rooster, or when I refused to let Elliott cut me from the team, or allow K.B. and Billy D. to burn me on the football field. The meaning of all these lessons from the past finally manifested. The stakes were a lot higher now. Fate had brought me to this particular point for some worthwhile reason and I was prepared to give it everything I had.

Things had unfolded in a way that allowed me to have many of those old coping mechanisms removed. Much pain remained, and I had to dig deep inside myself to go forward from this point. I had already hit my emotional bottom, so there was nothing to fear.

The new semester began with Medical Microbiology, Head and Neck, Neurobiology, and Introduction to Medicine. My first goal was to start rebuilding my self-esteem and self worth and replace the deadness I was feeling inside. There couldn't have been a better course than microbiology to start with. I had worked in microbiology for four years at my med tech job and I certainly knew this area well. There would only be one exam and my goal was to make honors. The grading system consisted of pass/fail/honors. The motto we were taught first semester was P = M.D, with. P meaning Pass. Courses were usually graded on a bell curve, with two standard deviations, which translated to 95% of the class passing and the remaining 5% receiving a score of Honors or Fail.

Making honors in a course was a big deal, one that could

really give my self-esteem a boost. I picked up my syllabus for Head and Neck Anatomy and Microbiology, then my Human Skull kit, and then retreated to my apartment, only to emerge for Head and Neck labs, where we dissected the last piece of cadaver. The only exception was Microbiology lectures, which were held two or three mornings a week, and the time I prepared a video tape of me interviewing a patient.

I knew the rules of the game now, which were simply to pass the exam by any means necessary. Just like in junior high sports, I knew that not letting up was the key to success. I stayed one or two lectures ahead in microbiology and put in extra time with the cadaver head and neck, prepared to learn every single detail. I would be over prepared this time. When the exam finally came, I confidently wrote my answers on the written test and turned in my paper, not allowing myself to even think about changing any answers. My heart beat hard as I prepared to go to the cadaver lab and start the practical exam. I knew what to expect this time. When the station rotation began, I made certain I saw where all the arrows on the floor were leading. I made sure to concentrate before recording the name for the tagged item. When the practical exam was over, I began to feel the panic and dysphoria I had felt after the first anatomy practical, on which I had choked so badly.

I sat in the corridor, waiting for the professor to review the correct answers to us; I no longer had arrogance and narcissism to hide behind. I had to bare this anxiety without any buffer. It was terrible, waiting there and knowing that this was do or die for my career in medicine. I began to think the worst; I knew I had failed. I found it hard to believe in myself.

When the answers finally became available, I was elated to find out that about 85% of my answers were correct. I also did very well on the written exam. It was such a wonderful feeling. I could now focus on microbiology, which I did. I kept a low profile during labs, in order to avoid situations that would frustrate me. I tried to just keep quiet, even though most of the labs were review of stuff I had been doing for years. I had learned the previous semester that my knowledge was not considered valid in this milieu, so I made an effort to be reticent.

I made an 85 on the exam; I wanted to make a 100. There were only a few questions that I didn't know the answer to. It would have taken a 92 to have made honors. At least I passed comfortably, so I wasn't too disappointed.

My patient interview was superb. It was critiqued in our weekly group meeting. Dr. Norfleet sent a letter of commendation to the Dean, which was to become part of my permanent record, commenting that it was one of the most outstanding he had ever seen. It was to be used in the future as a teaching model. It was hard to believe how much things had changed in just a couple of months.

Things continued to get better. I received a scholarship from the Medical Society back in Sanford, that I wasn't expecting. I was still able to work some on the weekend, with the more manageable schedule. This made it possible for me to pay my rent and car payment without financial strain. I made sure to maintain my ties with Roberts Chapel Baptist Church back home, where I taught drama and wrote plays for production, under the guidance of Pastor Sampson Buie, Jr.

From this point on, things continued to go well for me, except for one course that gave me a scare. Medical Statistics was a curriculum requirement. I thought I was through with math courses, but I wasn't. It would have been a shame to lose everything over such a relatively insignificant course. Statistics is important in medicine, in that the doctor has to know how to interpret clinical trials of various treatments and understand basic epidemiology. Few medical specialties require the physician to have a detailed knowledge of statistics. This particular course was taught at the Master's level by very knowledgeable instructors.

I felt as if a ghost from the past were returning to destroy me, just like in my dreams. I don't know if it was the attention deficit or what, but mathematics had always been my nemesis. Numbers require such precision and accuracy and there is no room for even the slightest error. My mind works in a more abstract and creative manner. Fortunately, Dr. Yankaskis was understanding and was willing to help me get through this final obstacle successfully. As a compensatory gesture, I did receive an honors grade for my elective course, The Red Blood Cell. At last, the time had come for clinical clerkships, a chance to interact with real patients and to start feeling what being a real physician is about.

CHAPTER 23

I'm Not Really a Doctor, I Just Play one at UNC

I don't recall exactly what it was, but I do know that, as we drove down I-40 East toward Raleigh, Vernon was complaining about something loud enough to hurt my ears. Obstetrics and Gynecology was foreign to both of us, but this would be our first clinical rotation.

Wake Medical Center was one of the largest hospitals in the area and a well-known training program for residents and students from UNC Hospitals. I wasn't sure what to expect, but I was so thrilled about finishing the basic science part of training that I didn't really care. Working with people was something with which I had always felt comfortable and I welcomed whatever lay ahead. We finally found the right building and began our orientation.

It was common knowledge that part of our grade came from enthusiasm and making our resident supervisor's life easier. There would be opportunities to work with several interns and residents, but I was to spend most of the first few weeks with a perky young first-year resident named Brita. I think she may have been from Pennsylvania or somewhere like that. She wore a short haircut and had a somewhat high-pitched voice. She was very easy to talk to and was a hard worker. I felt comfortable around her. Almost immediately, I was in a pair of scrubs facing a woman in stirrups and in labor, ready to push. This was exciting and I couldn't wait to see the birthing process for the first time.

Brita checked the cervical dilatation and said, "You're 13 centimeters ma'am. Your baby should be here soon." She then looked at me and said, "She's all yours Ken."

I'm sure the shock showed on my face, since I was expecting at least to see a delivery before doing one. Apparently, it didn't work that way. It was time for an Oscar-worthy performance, because I only knew what I remembered from readings. I was glad that my self-confidence had been restored and I took my place on the stool and prepared to catch, as Brita gave me play-by-play instructions. I soon learned that the key to a successful, uncomplicated, spontaneous vaginal delivery was lowering the head of the infant and allowing the top shoulder to slip under the pubic region. Once this had occurred, you were home free. It just felt so strange pulling on the head. I couldn't help but imagine the infant's head coming off.

Nature designed the process of assisting the new life coming in the world to not be rocket science. After a few deliveries, I had the hang of it. The hardest thing was holding on to the slippery joker and cutting the umbilical cord at the same time. The most fascinating part was seeing the newborn trying to adjust its vision as it peered around the room, a totally new world for it. That was always an exciting moment.

As always, it was only a matter of time before the ever-present subject of race had to be faced. I was starting to accept that being an ambassador for the black race was just going to be a role I would be stuck with indefinitely, so why not make the best of it. The perfect opportunity arose when a young, rural Caucasian couple came in for services. The father-to-be was perfectly cast as the personification of a *stars and bars* good old boy.

Uncle D.W., back in Goldston, had told me stories of how, during his youth, they were forced to look the other way if a white girl was within visual range. Failure to do so could result in a cruel and unusual punishment. Now, just a generation later, I was getting ready to engage in a procedure that would require me to touch the genital region of, heaven forbid, a young white woman and I couldn't help but wonder if I would be thrown out of the room, or maybe be lynched, once the baby was delivered. Absurd as it may sound, that form of thinking was not inconceivable for most young southern black men. As fate would have it, there was a complication with this case. Though minor, a superficial blood vessel was broken in the infant's scalp, causing an ugly hematoma.

This was just what I needed to happen. My intern and I handled the situation courteously and professionally, reassuring the young couple that this usually was not a serious problem and that the infant was perfectly healthy otherwise. To my surprise, the father actually thanked me before the baby was taken out to the nursery. There was a sense of accomplishment in being a participant in the process of birth, as well as participating in the symbolic death of racism.

There were occasional times when I was asked to leave the room by the mother or father, but I kept in mind that I was there for an education. This behavior was just a part of that education and not to be taken personally.

Medical students were not highly thought of by many professionals. Once, I really got jumped on by an O.R. Tech for touching her instruments, while assisting with a C-section. She was like a rabid dog. I didn't do that again. Many nurses devalued my existence by making it clear that they requested a *real doctor.* When these situations happened, I had to remember my mother saying, "They're jealous of you." Whether that was true or not, it was a way of coping.

It was my intention to stay on the high road. Thoughts of the incident at the Ham House were ever-present to remind me of what I was capable of, if pushed too far. That experience had instilled in me that there is nothing worth *losing it* over. I had chosen, or been chosen for, this path for a reason that was much greater than being bothered by damage to my ego. My first semester of med school had essentially cured me of those parts of my personality that were capable of over- reacting, acting too impulsively and in ways that could harm my future. Clearly, there had been reasons for everything that had happened to me over the years. This training of personality and spirit continued, even during this particular rotation, when a medical student was required to hold a retractor for what seemed like hours during a surgical procedure, or hold up the leg of a 300-pound patient to help give the operator a clear working field for a vaginal hysterectomy, which is a time consuming procedure.

Medical school was probably designed from the very beginning to teach humility. In my case, due to my stubbornness, there just needed to be more intense measures, which always seemed to occur when necessary.

The chief resident, Judy, was an African American woman, and one of the professors, Gerald, was of Jamaican descent. I'm sure that was a major frustration for all the racists on the scene. Our mentors met with Vernon and me one day over these exact matters. There had never been, in the history of the department, this many blacks in one place at one time, except for maybe housekeeping. This change guaranteed scrutiny for Vernon and me. Vernon had a knack for saying the wrong thing at the wrong time, usually due to naiveté, and he had major difficulties with this rotation. Furthermore, into the 6-week rotation, I began to shine and was able to impress my new intern with my skills in sewing up lacerations in the birth canal of one patient. It just so happened that this intern was a woman and, I suppose growing up with so many women around, I have always been more comfortable around women...unless, of course, it was a romantic situation.

I maintained my drive, worked on the new computer program for obstetrics, and was well prepared for my end-of-course oral exam. The professor could not trick or mislead me and I passed easily. My overall experience in OB-Gyn was encouraging.

The next stop was UNC Hospitals for internal medicine. This would be an 18-week rotation, divided into three six week parts: two General Medicine rotations and Nephrology.

Internal Medicine was known for its cerebral giants and the greatest fear on this rotation was being asked a question by your attending and not knowing the answer. (This form of questioning was referred to as *pimping*.) I witnessed a student who was a blue chip—son of a well-known doctor—try to bullshit an attending and the latter made an example out of student by embarrassing him silly. The point was, if you don't know the answer, then say "I don't know."

I began on the Nephrology service, where I worked with Annie, a very nice Puerto Rican intern. The supervising resident was a Jewish guy named Bob, who had a super sense of humor and was very nice to work with. Some nights on call, while we were assessing an emergency transferred patient, and he would comment, "They shipped this patient here thinking he would receive the highest quality of care from a tertiary medical center, and he gets you and me." I thought that was so funny and I would think of that every time I saw a patient for the first time. It was really cool to associate with some of the world-class attending physicians, but also quite intimidating for a third year medical student.

I recall working up my first patient and starting to prepare for presentation to the attending, which happened on the following morning at sit down rounds. I barely slept that night and Bob encouraged me by telling me there was nothing to worry about. In his own words, in a kidding manner, he said, "I've given plenty of shitty presentations. You'll have plenty of chances."

Internal Medicine presentations were nothing like the abbreviated presentations in OB-Gyn. Medicine Attendings wanted a concise but accurate job, preferably from memory. They expected a comprehensive differential diagnosis and detailed suggestions for the treatment plan. After presenting, you could expect to be asked questions pertaining to any aspect of the diagnosis given to the patient, as well as justifying the chosen treatment. My first presentation was not very memorable, so I must not have screwed up too badly.

As with most rotations to come, there were gunners on the team. A gunner is a student who makes it hard on other students, due to their excellent performances on tests and during rounds. On the other hand, they gave the average students something to aspire to be. These students were your future cardiologists, dermatologists, ear nose and throat specialists (E.N.T.), orthopedists, and other sub-specialists. Some of them were smarter than the interns with whom they worked. (Again, I acknowledge that if I ever need a heart transplant or brain surgery, these are the doctors I want doing it. I wouldn't want most of them for a family doc or therapist though, because they may over-diagnose or bore me to death.)

For primary care physicians, traits such as compassion, understanding, and interpersonal skills are more important than a mastery of esoteric medical knowledge. To the vast majority of the general public, the etiology of ischemic cardiomyopathy, necrotizing fasciaitis, or the most convenient route to the sella tursica is not that important. Patients are more concerned about how much time the doctor spends with them, or that their condition was explained in a manner they can understand, and having a positive outcome.

The next rotation was General Medicine, at Moses Cone Hospital in Greensboro. Cone is one of many Area Health Education Centers (A.H.E.C.) across the state. The patients were usually much less complex here and the Attendings more user friendly. This rotation made me want to be a Family Practitioner. Here, a medical student was at least shown the respect deserved. Back at UNC Hospitals, the nurses often treated students as expendable. There were times I could feel in the air the contempt many nurses had for students. I suppose they felt they needed to get their punches in while they could, because these students would one day be giving them orders and making four times their salary. Sometime even the ward clerks had tried to pull rank on me.

It was not like this at Cone. Students were viewed as doctors in training, and given respect similar to interns. There also was less competing between students and interns. Cone Hospital was closer to the real world than UNC Hospitals.

That month–and-a-half flew by and, before I knew it, I was back in Chapel Hill for the final medicine rotation, which was also General Medicine. I hated every minute of it. I had a good old boy from South Carolina for an intern. I'm trying hard to minimize the use of dirty words, but sometimes you just can't avoid it. This guy's attitude blatantly said to me, "Fuck you." I had come too far to let this make me behave inappropriately, so I played the role of scut monkey to a tee. Whatever he wanted, I did for him. Boy, I really had changed! The pre-med school me would have never tolerated so much, and even the attending asked me if this guy was stealing my thunder. The supervising resident was a beautiful woman from Egypt who often spent time with me and was helpful. That seemed to be the only good thing to happen through the whole rotation, which left a bad taste in my mouth. Its end was welcomed.

The next clerkship was Pediatrics. I was assigned an infant, Byron, who had been abandoned by his parents and temporarily adopted by the hospital. The Attending Pediatrician affectionately referred to him as Lord Byron. The baby had some serious problems with his cardio-respiratory system, but appeared healthy in general. Some days, I would go by the nursery and hold him in the rocking chair. In general, I wasn't very compatible with pediatrics and saw no chance of a career in the specialty.

The first day of rounds caught me off-guard because it was walk rounds to the bedside. I was expecting sit-down rounds, where it was easier to organize your presentation. I had just worked up a new infant patient. Before going into the room, the treating physician or medical student was required to briefly present the case to the group of about twenty people. When my turn came, I totally blanked. Had you asked me my name, I wouldn't have known. I just couldn't think and I felt the panic surging throughout my body. The intern, Harold, stepped in for me, but that moment left me feeling so embarrassed. Had I known at the time, I probably would have blamed it on A.D.D., but I'm glad I didn't know about it. Even though I could not focus and organize my work well, situations like that kept me focused on the larger goal: Staying true to the people I would one day treat and help. My ego stayed in check.

I had only one racial encounter during this rotation, and it wasn't that blatant. There was one attending who was made from the same mold as Senator Trent Lott. This doctor took it upon himself to make derogatory inferences that seemed directed primarily toward me. I was convinced that I would not allow such people to affect me.

The best way to beat such people is by being as successful as possible, which is just what I've done. I was blessed with the ability to compromise and negotiate in times of racial conflict. I was already a psychiatrist at heart; I just hadn't been trained yet. I already knew how to make an instant and accurate assessment of what a person thought of me, just by interacting with that person for a few moments. That's what helped me navigate through all the racial mines planted in the sea of medical training.

My friend Vernon was not so fortunate. It seems that, in order to survive in such a competitive and political environment as medical school, any lack of surplus intellectual assets *must* be replaced by interpersonal skills. Making a bad first impression in front of powerful people can be fatal; the key to survival is playing off of your positive traits. Vernon had a problem in the interpersonal skills area, which led to him be eaten alive on his neurology rotation. His dreams came to a sudden halt. I did what I could to give him support, but I had to focus hard, since precedence had been set, and I didn't want to be the next casualty.

Most students who start medical school finish medical school. Along the way, a significant amount of students fall by the wayside, like casualties of war. Medical schools attract some of the brightest minds on earth, although a minimum competency level for practicing medicine has been a bit ambiguous and never been precisely established, except for state licensing examination scores. Today's students must pass their national board exam to qualify for licensure, which is fair. For me, it would have been tragic not to have had the opportunity to sit for boards because of someone's political agenda, narcissism, or racist beliefs. My next rotation would change the path of my life forever.

CHAPTER 24

Intro to Psychiatry

Somewhere Over the Rainbow

I had heard stories about Dorothea Dix Hospital and Camp Butner, two of the state's four mental hospitals. They didn't sound like places you'd want to go.

Few students look forward to the Psychiatry rotation and those lectures were poorly attended the previous year. The psychiatry rotation is not optional. Another student and I, who shared a dark blue Chevy Cavalier owned by the state, arrived on the campus of Dorothea Dix Hospital (D.D.H.) around 8:45 a.m. It resembled a small university, with numerous red brick buildings and vast lawns and shade trees. After a short drive, we came upon a large yellow building. The entrance area appeared to have been recently renovated. Attached to this building was a perpendicular extension that was three stories high, running from far behind the entrance building to a considerable distance in the front. The back portion was known as the Adult Unit, which was divided into three portions, determined by the three floors. I was assigned to 1A, which was divided into a male and female ward.

The first day was primarily for orientation. Our group consisted of about eight students, six being future surgeons or internal medicine docs and one a pediatrician. Most were a few years younger than I. The group also had two or three comedians, so there was always entertainment when we went to lunch every day. All of us were coming off very intense rotations, such as Medicine or Surgery, so the change to psychiatry was like a break. The pace was much slower and formalities weren't such a big deal. You weren't even required to wear a tie. (Although the real reason was that an agitated patient could grab that tie and choke you to death.)

After a short lecture about the dangers of losing them and causing a breach in security, we were given our own set of keys. The door to the patient ward was constructed of metal and unbreakable glass and made a characteristic slamming sound when closed. The ward was ancient, but clean, well-lit, and very solid in structure. The patients usually didn't know the difference between a student and an attending physician, so we all got honorary promotions, good only for this rotation.

Walking further down the hallway, we saw a room with smoke coming out the door, as if it were on fire. The person orientating us didn't look concerned. As we walked by the door, we noticed six or seven patients smoking cigarettes, like there was no tomorrow. We soon learned that nearly all of the more severe mental patients were addicted to nicotine. Most would rather miss a meal than miss a smoke break. It seemed as though, if a patient were in a coma and a smoke break were announced over the P.A. system, that patient would instantly become conscious and get in line for a smoke.

We visited the nursing station, commonly referred to as the fish bowl, because it was surrounded by glass. Many patients just stood outside, looking in for no particular reason, watching various staff do their paper work. In the station, I saw Dr. Eaton, who was at WSSU at the same time I was. We had a few science classes together and he had become an attending physician since finishing his residency. He had been a good role model for people like me.

Most of the other students wanted a good grade, but weren't really interested in psychiatry. As for me, I was fascinated. I felt more at home in this ancient structure than at any other time during my training. All of the drama a person could handle was right there. Some behaviors and situations evoked laughter, and I learned that laughter was a coping mechanism to avoid shedding tears, or to keep one's spirits up enough to deal with a particular situation.

We were assigned a few patients of our own, to work up and follow their treatment until discharged. I had heard that a new medicine called Prozac was available and I wanted a chance to see its effects and worked directly with Dr. Friedman, an attending, formerly from New York. Students were allowed to attend emergency screenings of patients involuntarily committed from one of several counties in the catchment area. These evaluations were done by a resident psychiatrist. There was no way of telling what might present next. I found the element of surprise and danger quite intriguing, when most students did not. There was always excitement in the air, especially when the alarm went off and P.I.C. major was announced over the intercom. P.I.C. major meant a patient was out of control and all manpower available needs to get there STAT! Those staff members involved were specially trained to take the patient down without causing major harm. The patient would then be given an injection of Haldol and Ativan and would usually require seclusion and restraint. P.I.C. minors usually meant a patient was starting to escalate and that, without immediate intervention, violent behavior was imminent.

Each student was required to present a report on a major psychiatric illness and a case presentation of a patient of his or her choice. I chose substance abuse and did a fair job. The addictive potential of cocaine was interesting. I learned that lab mice addicted to cocaine had experimentally been given a choice between food and water or cocaine and had all chosen the cocaine. Due the lack of a cerebral cortex, they all continued using the cocaine until death.

My case presentation was on post-traumatic stress disorder. I felt a lot of compassion for women who had survived incest, rape, or physical and emotional abuse. Before this rotation, I had never seriously thought about a career in psychiatry. From this point forward, however, there was conflict of whether to choose Family Medicine or Psychiatry. There were aspects I liked about both specialties and I had several months before a commitment was required.

I was beginning to see the light at the end of the tunnel. It was looking like it was really going happen, that nothing could stop me now. One more rotation and I'd be a senior student.

At this point, I wasn't committed to psychiatry. Even if I had been, I wasn't ready to come out. It was hard to find anyone who'd say anything good about the specialty. It was not uncommon to hear residents from other specialties trash Family Practice, so just think what would have happened had I mentioned psychiatry! At that time, I didn't know enough about psychiatry to defend it.

The Department of Psychiatry at UNC Hospitals took an active role by inviting interested students to come talk with the residents. I decided to attend and quickly discovered that I had been lied to, concerning the type of people in psychiatry. The residents and some of the attendings were extremely nice, and nobody was anywhere near as crazy as I had heard. I was probably the craziest one there.

Score one for psychiatry.

❧

Before I could move on, I had to complete the surgery rotation. I was assigned to Urology for six weeks, Trauma Surgery for six weeks, Ear, Nose, and Throat for two weeks, and Orthopedic Surgery for the remainder of the time. Each rotation was interesting and exciting. The Attendings seemed to enjoy teaching students. I knew I could never be a surgeon because they round too much. They have pre-rounds, then morning rounds, then grand rounds, then pre-evening rounds, then X-Ray rounds, and finally evening rounds. I wouldn't' have been surprised to know they then dreamed about rounds. Up at 5:00 am and home at 8:00 pm. On those nights with call duty, they had to prepare to be up all night and then all the next day. I could never, ever adjust to such a lifestyle, being the late sleeper I am. In the operating room, it was always interesting.

One Urology attending must have had Tourette's, because he seemed to be incapable of not saying "goddamit!" and yelling at staff. It seemed that every time he operated, he cut an artery and had a tantrum.

The highlights of the Surgery rotation were putting my hands inside the body cavity and feeling the internal organs of a motor vehicle accident patient during exploratory surgery. The Chief Resident allowed me the honor of operating the scalpel and excising the gallbladder, with another case. The low point of the rotation was holding those damn legs in the Orthopedics operating room. That job could go on for hours and it always turned out to be an obese person needing the hip replacement. The overall experience was great, however, because I learned that the stereotypical surgeon is a myth. Some of the nicest doctors I met were surgeons.

CHAPTER 25

What's Up Doc?

Who Me?...Yeah, Me!

The atmosphere was much more laid back for fourth year medical students, since the initiation into medicine is completed throughout third year medical school. The objective in this last year was to get accepted into the residency program of choice, while taking enough one-month electives to stay busy for the entire ten months. Getting into the residency program of choice involves the national match program, in which the residents rank their desired program, just as each program ranks the residents they want in their programs. Historically, UNC Hospitals medical students match up with their first choice of residency program almost 90% percent of the time. Only the top medical schools can match this impressive statistic.

We students had through November to interview with the residency programs that were our top choices. All students had a few top choices, but interviewed with other schools to learn more about their programs, provide a backup plan, or just to be wined and dined. Specialties that were most competitive included Dermatology, ENT, Radiology, and Ophthalmology. These programs and a few others commonly had more applicants than positions, so applicants stood a chance of not always getting their top choice. Most applicants were the gunners I spoke of previously. Less competitive specialties, in the primary care arena, sometimes had trouble filling all of their residency positions. Psychiatry residency programs depended on their reputations and educational resources. Our program traditionally tended to give preferential treatment to students from its medical school. The dean's office assisted students with their applications and personal statements and we were reminded of the importance of the interview.

Residents handle the majority of the doctor workload at all teaching institutions because they're very affordable for the hospital and they make the Attending's job easier and more prestigious. In exchange, the residents get to benefit from the Attending's knowledge and hone their skills with the massive amount of patients passing continuously through the hospital system. Medical students donate their services free, and actually pay for the opportunity to be taught enough medicine to become a resident. It is a win-win situation for all involved. The main criticism of residency training has been the long on-call hours that often force the resident to care for patients with compromised ability to function cognitively. This is believed to increase the occurrence of errors made by residents. Efforts are underway today to rectify that problem.

My academic year started in July or August, 1991. Students were encouraged to take electives that were totally unrelated to their planned specialty, since there would be years ahead in which to train. I signed up for Neurology Clinic and Outpatient Medicine Clinic at Cone, and Consult Liaison Psychiatry, Forensic Psychiatry, and a couple of others. I still hadn't made a choice between Family Medicine and Psychiatry. I had done a little research on the field of psychiatry and no longer minded saying that I was considering it. Psychiatry was appealing, but I wanted to be able to do more medicine in the traditional manner. In family medicine, the pace was so fast that it wouldn't allow the holistic approach I desired.

I decided to do a rotation in family medicine before deciding. I did this with an AHEC center in Fayetteville, NC. It was all outpatient clinics, consisting primarily of treating hypertension, diabetes, infections, injuries, and preventive medicine. It was not a bad experience. The Attendings were nice to work with and they actually tried to recruit me. It was such a different experience, to be valued and wanted.

Family practice was good, but I still felt something was missing and time was running out.

Dr. Lindsey was a young Geriatric Psychiatrist on faculty at UNC Hospitals and he became my main resource for psychiatry residency. He was very upbeat and honest and went over all the benefits of going into psychiatry. It began to sound better and better. In addition, he told me that my chances of acceptance into the program at University of NC Hospitals were very good. University of NC Hospitals Psychiatry Residency Program was one of the best in the country and accepted 12-14 first year residents each year. Most programs had fewer residents. This one offered training in psychodynamic psychiatry, as well as psychopharmacology or, in layman's terms, therapy and drugs. Many programs were moving away from traditional psychotherapy, probably in preparation for our current mental health predicament. It's much more cost efficient to give a patient a pill and have them come back a month later, for a 15-minute follow-up visit, than to see them once or twice weekly for therapy sessions.

University of NC Hospital's residency program continued to value psychoanalysis and its many branches of therapeutic approaches. It has been proven that the most effective psychiatric treatment is a combination of psychotherapy and medications. The psychiatrists of the future will need to be skilled in both of those areas.

It wasn't long before I made my decision to go for the psychiatry residency, with the University of NC Hospitals program as my first choice. I went on interviews to Duke and Bowman Gray, but really had no interest. I think I went because neither school even bothered to allow me to visit, when I was applying to medical school, and I didn't want to miss any chance at turning them down. What goes around does come around. Some of the residents at Duke were very unhappy and were making plans to leave. If I remember correctly, Duke couldn't even fill all of their positions that year. Moreover, I never wanted to be a part of such an arrogant establishment. Match day comes every March and is the most exciting day of the senior student's year, except for graduation day. I knew that University of NC Hospitals wanted me in their program, so I felt some relief, but not surprise, when my envelope was opened and read aloud. Nationwide, there was a shortage of African American psychiatrists, especially males. Again, it was a strange feeling to be in demand and desired.

This was really happening. I understood even better what all that marching and suffering during the sixties was all about: It was for people like me to have a fair chance.

Regardless of how intelligent one is, without the highest quality undergraduate and high school education, competition with the so-called gunners could not be expected. However, I give credit to my medical school for allowing me to have a fair chance. I always had the potential, but the real question was whether the school was willing to compensate for those factors for which I wasn't responsible. I don't mean affirmative action; I mean simply recognizing my true potential. It was just like what Coach Elliott did for some of the Caucasian boys back on the middle school teams. Some became very good athletes, inferiority was never a factor. Black boys in that day focused on sports at an early age because they had access to little else. Basketball abilities were a way of saying, "I'm good at this and nobody can tell me different." The ones who weren't good at some sport often fared poorly and they were ridiculed by their peers for trying to develop academic skills. This is where I came from. This was my reality.

I became the first man in my family to even go to college. No ancestor of mine could have attended a prestigious institution of higher learning before the 1960's, regardless of qualifications or desire. That was not reality for them. I can safely say that most of my medical school classmates did not share that same reality and I'm sure that academic excellence was encouraged throughout their education. Some had three or four generations of doctors in the family, whereas nobody in the history of my family had ever even known a doctor on a personal level. Many classmates had the advantage of their parents taking an active role along their educational path and it was their right to carry on the tradition. Also in the spirit of tradition, when a couple of qualified blacks that aren't straight-A students get into medical school or law school, it is often labeled as affirmative action by the ignorant, as though they were given something they didn't deserve. What a person has to overcome to even be qualified may not be taken into consideration.

I think a lesson in living can sometimes be more valuable than the A that a student may receive in zoology or geology, at a prestigious university. A lesson in living also has much more practical value, but is usually given no positive consideration by the rule makers. People who have never had to struggle in life often cannot appreciate these facts. I suppose these people assume that blacks should be satisfied just being allowed to be called an American, and not even try to compete at all with groups having no history of *government-sponsored* discrimination. Most blacks have never had a dream of going back to 1776 and starting over, equal to other Americans. Most of the damage came after 1865, when reconstruction laws were ignored and the Jim Crow system implemented. Opponents to *all* affirmative action would suggest that we just forget this ever happened. I for one will never forget it. Furthermore, it is easy to suggest and to say, now that everybody supposedly has equal opportunity. For over a hundred years, whites had a 100% chance of acceptance for whatever program or life path they chose. There can be no greater affirmative action than 100% to zero percent. Anyone in their right mind knows that without some form of pressure, not only would blacks not be treated fairly by those in power, but would be driven back to slavery—if there were a way to do that. If we waited for people to do the right thing as the only means of rectifying the past, the country would never have moved past 1968, in regard to the racial problem.

CHAPTER 26

Life as a Psychiatry Resident

It's Hard But It's Fair

May 10, 1992. This was the day my name changed again. I had never been to a medical school graduation, much less been in one, but strangely I didn't really feel that excited. Lawrence had made a surprise appearance a couple of days before. We spent some time together and he went to rehearsal with me, but had to leave for Jacksonville before the actual ceremony, leaving behind blown up posters of Dr. King and Malcolm X.

It was a beautiful sunny Sunday morning and my family started to gather outside of my apartment. Phyllis was home from Rochester. Due to the distance, her trips home were reserved for special occasions, so I was glad to see her. Even Otis was able to come. Eventually, we made it to Memorial Auditorium, on the university campus, located near the Old Well, which is almost an icon (due to being photographed so many times in association with the university). Just sixteen years earlier, I had been in Upward Bound on this very campus, a naïve kid clueless about life. Today, I was receiving my Doctor of Medicine degree. In the words of boxing promoter Don King, *Only in America* could this be true.

I was not able to comprehend the magnitude of what was about to happen. I didn't seem to get too excited, probably because I had focused so hard and for so long on this day. It was difficult to believe it was really happening

I did start to feel a little pumped as we marched into the building in pairs. There were so many people in the building that I felt anonymous. My family and minister were hidden in the crowd and I just went with the flow. Before I knew it, the school was ready to pass out the diplomas. There were about 150 students lined up in alphabetical order, so it took a little while. Walking across the stage was much like being a dream, a dream in which I felt myself purged of all the frustrations and disappointments of the previous years. And then, as I returned to my seat, there was a feeling of euphoria.

All the diplomas were distributed and we prepared for the final ceremonial element. The tassels were flipped and, just like that, we were all doctors for life. They couldn't take it back. Caps headed for the ceiling and then we began marching out to Pomp and Circumstance, played by the orchestra.

Alfreda gave me a cookout at her house, well attended by relatives and friends. Gwen and I were still together and we were able to spend a little time together after things had died down. I had agreed to give the Men's Day address on the third Sunday in June at Roberts Chapel. I wanted it to be good, so I spent a lot of time writing and rehearsing over the next weeks. Residency training would not officially begin until the first of July. We were advised to try to have as much fun as possible over the next weeks, because there would never be a break this long again. That turned out to be true.

The word *intern* is no longer used, being replaced by the politically correct *First Year Resident* or PGY-1 (Post Graduate Year). The name may have changed, but the game is still the same. There were 12 PGY-1 residents in our class, so the usual plan was to divide into three groups and rotate every four months. On call, coverage would be once every three to four nights. My first rotation was Inpatient Psychiatry at University of NC Hospitals. Home base was an ancient building that had a date with a demolition crew three years later. It was known as South Wing. The average patient load per resident was 3-

10 patients, depending how unlucky you were on your on call day and night. The average day started with rounds at 9:00 am in the conference room, where we reviewed each patient with the Attending. Once a week there would be special rounds with every member of the treatment team present, in order to develop or review treatment plans. A good medical student could be very helpful by helping trim down a resident's workload. They knew that you could put in a good word to the Chief Resident, in regard to their end of rotation grade. After rounds, it was time to go to the patient's rooms for the daily assessment, to be documented in the form of a progress note in the patient's chart. After lunch, there were usually lectures, group, or supervision.

If a patient comes in and you are on call, you report immediately to the emergency room or crisis clinic, with a second year resident and your medical student. The PGY-1 does the bulk of the work, if there is not more than one patient. The PGY-2 is there for back up and supervision, since s/he went through this the first year. Once the assessment is completed, the Attending may be called on the phone to discuss the details of the case. The Attending encourages you to take the initiative and he/she will approve of your plan, unless it is inappropriate. Usually, you won't need to even call the Attending unless you plan to release the patient, because the case will be discussed during morning rounds. Many of the Emergency Room cases are on an involuntary commitment and the overall purpose of the first or second assessment (known as a qualified physician's exam) is to determine if they are imminently dangerous to themselves or others, as determined by North Carolina law. Two examiners must agree before a patient can legally be kept against their will. Most involuntarily committed patients will be upset, making the assessment more difficult. As a rule of thumb, the patient is admitted if there is any doubt about their safety or any chance of them causing harm to others.

Another less useful rule of thumb about patients is that those who most need to be in the hospital do not wish to be there, whereas those who do not need to be in the hospital want to stay as long as possible. Prior to mental health reform, potentially violent patients were routinely sent to one of the state hospitals. The future plan is for the community to handle their own problem patients locally. Another interesting rule of thumb is, do *not* under any circumstances, believe a word a cocaine or narcotic addict says. No! They do not really want to stop; they want to stop for now. They have become so accustomed to lying that they no longer know the truth. Despite good intention, the trainee eventually realizes that their time and emotion are limited resources and everyone does not really want help in the same way the doctor wants to help them. Trying to cure everyone can burn a doctor out quickly; some psychiatric patients are emotionally draining.

On the not-on-call days, the resident may be on the way home by 5:00 pm. A day of call lasts 24 hours, usually 8:00 am to 8:00 am the next day. On call will make one think again about that full moon myth and being followed by black clouds. I have experienced both.

T.G. was a PGY-2 who was very skilled as a therapist and now practices near Asheville, N.C. Every time T.G. and I were on call together, it was guaranteed to be holy hell. One time, the moon was full and we were pulling call duties together. It started around 6:00 pm and was still going strong at 6:00 am the next day, with not a wink of sleep that night. In addition, nursing was so angry that I was run out of the nursing station. I think we had eight back-to-back admissions. There is no worse feeling than going to rounds the next morning without having had any sleep. Sometimes, instead of exhaustion, you may feel a bit hypo-manic, which means speeded up and silly. Everything seems especially funnier than usual. Even on the nights that you get a chance to sleep a little, there usually comes an interruption at around 3:00 am, and of the most annoying kind. Beep, beep, beep goes the beeper and an unfamiliar number is displayed. Your phase-2 sleep has been disrupted and it takes your eyes a moment to adjust to the light. And then the number is slowly entered into the phone.

"Hello, this is Dr. Headen, I understand you have an emergency, how can I help you?" "Is this Dr. Headen?"

"Yes it is. How can I help you?"

"Dr. Headen, I can't sleep."

That made two of us unable to sleep. I was sometimes convinced that there was a conspiracy in which these people were paid to call at two or three in the morning, whenever I was on call.

The best thing about psychiatry is that it's never boring. People who love dramatic arts love different characters. The Diagnostic and Statistical Manual (DSM-V) is the official bible for mental health professionals everywhere. All criteria for making a diagnosis are included here in organized fashion. There actually is a dramatic cluster of personality disorders commonly seen. The most challenging patients are those diagnosed with borderline personality disorder. They are ubiquitous, being found anywhere there are people. The single word that would describe one with this disorder would be *chaos*. They usually lead a chaotic lifestyle that may involve frequent suicide gestures, mood swings, depression, anxiety, motor vehicle accidents, unstable relationships, impulsive acts, fear of abandonment, and sexual orientation issues. These patients can transfer chaos to others, if there aren't clear boundaries. One of their favorite games is splitting people, which results in pitting one person against another. After a while, people unfamiliar with caring for them may start behaving unlike themselves, sometimes acting angry, irritable or anxious. The borderline patient seems to be pleased when this occurs. Patients with this diagnosis can be manipulative. They see the world as black or white, with no gray areas. They may love you one minute and hate you the next. There is a burning rage within. The biggest problem is the tendency for self-injurious behaviors and suicide attempts.

The next personality is the *histrionic*. These patients have been described as the Scarlet O'Hara type or damsel in distress. A good single word description would be *superficial*. This word was chosen because, after all the dust settles, nothing has been accomplished. Histrionic patients have to be the center of attention constantly. They use dramatic descriptions for everything they talk about and they tend to embellish. Frequently, there are times when they are seductive. They may be more prone to teasing behaviors than sexual acting out. These patients are seen for treatment on occasion, usually for depression, anxiety, or somatic complaints.

Narcissistic Personality disorder is common, but most are too vain or oblivious to everyone else's reality to present for treatment. *Conceited* is the simplest description. The name comes from the Greek mythical figure Narcissus, who drowned accidentally, due to being obsessed with his reflection from a deep pool of water. These patients feel that the world revolves around them and they are incapable of feeling empathy for others. Their only concern is for their own well-being. These patients claim to be more than they really are and will accept undeserved credit without concern. They may claim to know famous or powerful people. Criticism is *never* taken well and may evoke intense anger.

Similar to the narcissistic personality is the *Anti-Social* Personality Disorder, or Sociopathic. The name does not mean not liking to socialize with others, as some readers may be thinking. Anti-socials can be found at the local jail being bailed out by their mother or girlfriend. They can be very charming and then they bite like a rattlesnake. They feel empty inside and have no concept of how others feel or why laws exist. They can be good at faking pity or pretending to feel things they don't really feel. They feel no remorse, but are usually remorseful about being caught. One study found this class not to be the brightest criminals, because they would frequently make some stupid mistake that would foil their crime. An example might be a robber who is caught by using his real drivers' license for identification before holding up the cashier. These type mistakes were found to be commonplace for the average sociopath by investigating forensic psychiatrists, suggesting perhaps damaged wiring within certain brain circuits. Their defense is usually predictable. It's always someone else's fault for their predicaments. A good one-word description would be thoughtless or *disrespectful*

Sometimes there is a *mixed* personality disorder, with any combination of these four disorders. There are two other clusters of personality disorder, *anxious* and *paranoid*. We all have some of traits mentioned in personality disorders. A personality *disorder* can only be diagnosed if the behavior leads to a pattern of undesirable consequences causing social or interpersonal dysfunction. The most common personality disorder diagnoses of the anxious and paranoid clusters include avoidant, dependent, obsessive-compulsive, passive, paranoid, schizoid, and schizotypal. These disorders will not be discussed here.

Four months went by quickly and then it was off to Dorothea Dix, the state hospital in Raleigh, NC. I was familiar with Dix from med school, so it was a lot like going home. The most difficult part was making that 30-mile drive daily. The most ill patients in the State were treated and housed at Dix and the atmosphere was less formal than at the university. The patient load was much heavier here, and most of the patients involuntary committed from across the state.

A careless doctor could easily get hurt working in this environment, so my adrenalin levels stayed up when admitting patients. I presented as being calm, but my *fight or flight* was always ready to kick in, if necessary. Once, on 1-A, I told a patient that she couldn't go home. The next thing I knew, there was a big black purse coming toward my head. I reacted beautifully and blocked it with the patient's chart. Interestingly, the other patients immediately came to my assistance and remained until the P.I.C. team arrived. I told my colleague, Nancy, that the patient couldn't hurt me because I was an athlete, and she found that to be quite humorous. I was serious!

There was one other time in the admissions office when a heavyset female patient became upset about having to come into the hospital. She charged at me like a linebacker and, fortunately, the officer tackled her before she made contact. For a moment, I almost had a flashback, thinking I was back on the football field.

Most of the time, I actually liked the excitement of the

mental health milieu. The workload was heavier than at the university—my all time record was fourteen admissions in one night. Who says Psychiatry is easy?

We were required to do a rotation of medicine while at Dix, caring for patients with mental and developmental disabilities. It was a serious rotation, and sometimes patients did die, as illustrated in the Introduction of this book. I was certified in advanced cardiac life support (ACLS) and I hoped to never have to use it. Fortunately, I never did have to attempt resuscitating anyone.

Most medical problems were common, like myocardial infarction, seizure disorders, infections, hypertension, thyroid disease, blocked bowels, or delirium. We worked directly under a Medicine Attending. The rotation was good for helping us get more accustomed to treating a variety of non-psychiatric conditions.

Eventually, I made it back to the University of NC Hospitals, where my next rotation was Neurology. The running joke about the three brain specialists had long been, Neurologists know it all yet do nothing, Neurosurgeons know nothing yet do it all, and Psychiatrists know nothing and do nothing. I am sure the author of the joke belonged to neither specialty. I had the impression that neurologists in general disliked psychiatrists, viewing us as pussies and not quite real doctors. This may have been because of what happened earlier in the year, when I ordered my first neurology consult. There was an overworked resident who began yelling and cursing into the phone when he heard the words *consult* and *spinal tap* in the same sentence. He suggested that he didn't have time to supervise any spinal tap and that I needed to do it my damn self. I kindly thanked him and informed my attending. We were eventually able to get a Neurology attending to come supervise the tap (which, incidentally, went beautifully). Because of that encounter with the resident, I have never felt comfortable asking for a neurology consultation.

My month on neurology went well. I had Dr. Vaughn for an Attending, who was very personable and easy to work with.

His favorite line was, "So, what do you want to do? What do you want to do with this patient?" One day, the attending who initiated Vernon's dismissal from med school did our walk rounds. Vernon had described him as a hybrid of Lucifer and the Anti-Christ, but I wasn't that impressed. Since I knew what he was capable of, I stayed on my toes. He tried the same question on me that he had used on Vernon: the effect of Magnesium on the reflex response. Very calmly, I gave the correct answer. The laugh was on him that day.

I finished my first year back on 4 South Adult Psychiatry and I was a little more comfortable this go 'round.

The start of PGY-2 was welcomed. Except for on call every 10-12 days, the entire year would be outpatient care. Finally, it was time for the lighter side of psychiatry. The resident's clinic was open to the public, in addition to those patients added during crisis clinic and inpatient follow-up care. The average day consisted of four or five therapy sessions, lectures, supervision, and crisis or psychopharmacology clinic. One day a week was assigned to an AHEC site. I was assigned to the Wilmington AHEC Center, which was about two hundred miles away. After driving the rental Ford Taurus wagon the 400 mile weekly round-trip proved unacceptably exhausting and inefficient with time, I, along with three other residents, got to fly there in one of the medical school's fleet of airplanes. The pilots were friendly and of the highest quality, and mechanical maintenance was excellent, so safety was not a concern. Fred, John, and Scott were several years younger than I was which seemed to always keep things fresh. Scott was the all-American handsome nice-guy, Fred was the Nordic transplant who was easy going and scholarly, and John was the party-guy who made his insatiable passion toward Asian women always the top issue of the day. We always had fun together. There was a young attending there, Dr. Kowalski, who was preparing to take his board exams and really enjoyed teaching us. We shot amateur video at the beach and Mental Health Center to the soundtrack of Inner Circles' *Bad*

Boys theme music from the TV show "Cops" that would later be used as part of a hilarious video compilation of our residency years for the entertainment segment of our future graduation ceremony at the end of our training. The patients we saw at the center were much like those seen at any mental health center. The primary focus was education, so the workload was light. We usually had our supervision as a group. Supervision by a more experienced doctor consisted primarily of picking apart a case or session for discussion and questions.

Back at the university, we were allowed to select our own supervisors, if they could accommodate. Dr. Hill, my first supervisor, was a versatile alumnus of the program who was very skilled in insight-oriented psychotherapy, among other things. His favorite word was *why*: "WHY? Why did you say that? Why did you do that? WHY, WHY, WHY?" When we first started, I didn't know why I was doing anything. I found it next to impossible to have a session with a patient, consisting of taking notes, listening, clarifying, confronting, interpreting, and experiencing the transference and counter-transference, which was all required for any case discussed in supervision. This would be a nightmare for any trainee with the mildest ADHD.

Therapy is one of those things that, the more it is done, the better you become at it. Learning the technique was initially extremely difficult. Over the years, it has become second nature. It is impossible to survive practicing psychiatry without the skill of being able to do three or four things very well simultaneously.

Dr. Soltys was a much older doctor and trained at Harvard in child and adult psychiatry. Many of the other residents weren't in tune with his style. Naturally, he became my favorite supervisor. He chose to be creative, by asking patients to describe what their life would be like if a miracle happened and instantly cured them with the stroke of a magic wand. This gave the patient an opportunity to conceptualize a target to shoot for. Every achievement begins with a simple thought. When a person is severely depressed, there are no longer any pleasant images within their random involuntary thoughts. Should a person refuse to participate in this simple exercise, the therapist can interpret a resistance to treatment. A return to health is not possible without conscious participation from the subject. Another technique involved totally agreeing with the depressed patient about their feelings, after listening to them complain for a few minutes. "Gosh, if all that had happened to me I would be depressed too." The goal was to help the patient balance all of those negative thoughts with some desirable thoughts about how they would wish things to be. It is common knowledge that a person with nothing to feel happy about cannot possibly be happy and sane at the same time. Step one to recovery is identifying with as many positive associations as possible.

I still use both techniques frequently in my practice today.

Another pearl Dr. Soltys left with me were the three types of patients who would be seen daily in the practice of psychiatry. First, there are those *just passing through*, whom you never see more than once or twice. Secondly are the *visitors* who come by more frequently, usually just for refills or in time of crisis. The third type of patient is the *consumer.* These patients are a delight to work with because they are glad to be there and follow instructions as directed. They never miss appointments and are always issue oriented. They also are unfortunately far and few between in the average general practice.

Every caseload had several borderlines onboard and all psychiatrists *must* be able to effectively deal with these challenging patients. I once had a patient reach into her purse and pull out a razor blade near the end of our session. She flashed it a couple of times to be certain I saw it, and then bolted out the door. This is where the fun and games really begin. You as a practicing psychiatrist *cannot!* I repeat, cannot, *ever* allow such behavior to go unchecked, so the appropriate authorities must be notified to help retrieve the patient, unless you don't mind being seen chasing a woman wielding a weapon all over the hospital campus. Such an act is usually worth a ticket for at least an overnight stay at the hospital. The counter-transference here usually isn't very positive. This always provides plenty to talk about during the next session.

Among all major diagnoses, only bipolar disorder and major depression patients have a higher suicide rate than borderline personality disorder, who attempt more but with less lethal intent and method. A large number of successful suicide deaths by borderline patients are miscalculated or accidental, and are cries for attention triggered by abandonment or rejection issues. High-risk behavior randomly translates into at least a few deaths just based on mathematical principals of basic statistics. Since record keeping started, the suicide rate has been in the approximate range of 30,000 per year with a large rise during the Great Depression and a slight increase during the recession of the 70's. The most reliable risk factors historically have been race white, sex male, age over 59, major loss/illness, alcohol abuse, divorced or single, and severely anxious or depressed mood. Black females have remained at the lowest risk, while teens of all races are on the rise for suicide completions. Due to the rising rate of malpractice litigation, many providers are opting to not treat any new patients with a history of frequent suicide attempts.

Terminating the therapeutic relationship when the doctor moves away, retires, or finishes training can be difficult for some patients. When the transference created is that of a parental figure, termination can trigger a strong fear of abandonment and separation anxiety in the patient. This is why it is recommended to allow plenty of sessions just for terminating the relationship. Patients have been known to make suicide attempts, engage in self-injurious behaviors, or other unhealthy acts, when this reaction takes effect. The therapist has to be able to set limits and boundaries and to follow through with involuntary commitment, when required. Sometimes, a contractual agreement at the commencement of treatment can have ground rules in place during times of crisis.

During my second year of residency, Gwen and I were having major relationship problems, which resulted in us finally calling it quits. She thought I had other relationships, but there was nothing serious between me and anyone else. Basically, we just weren't seeing things the same anymore and, even though there had been little there for some time, we continued to hang on too long. I just was not what she needed any longer and vice versa. This happens to many couples as they advance into their 30's. It was emotionally devastating to go through this break–up, to the point where, on some days, I felt as though I might die. She had her family for support. I talked to my sister, Alfreda, once or twice, but that was about it. I had started seeing a psychologist, Dr. Steve Mullinix, who helped me tremendously. I still meet with Steve today. I have highly valued our relationship and it has definitely taught me to be a better psychotherapist. Over the years, I have taken the opportunity to go back in time all the way to the beginning, and unload much of my baggage. If my purpose for going into psychiatry was to understand my own problems, then that has pretty much been accomplished. However, understanding and resolving are separate entities. I never could have begun writing this book, had I not processed and found peace and understanding with certain issues. I have found the process to be quite cathartic and I feel no shame. I strongly recommend to all who can afford it to explore your issues with a professional *if you are sincere and serious* about personal growth. If not, I strongly recommend not wasting your time and money or the time of the therapist. If you are sincere and serious about change, and willing to put the time and effort in, you will feel a lot better about yourself. Remember, *patience will be the key*. You will receive equal to that you put in. You did not land in your current state overnight and change will not come overnight.

There is no on call for PGY-3. Instead, I had to do a few months at the behavioral research unit at Dix. There were some personality conflicts with the nursing staff that contributed to unpleasantness for me, but the attending doctor was nice and no problem to work with. I was glad to finally get that rotation behind me.

Next was the Consult and Liaison rotation, which I really liked. I had spent several weeks on the service during fourth year medical school. Other specialties requested consultation, when they had a psychiatric question that needed an answer. The most difficult cases emotionally were in the burn unit, where some patients had become depressed after sustaining disfiguring burn injuries. These were very courageous patients. Such an injury really forces the patient to look inside for strength.

The most common consult patients were for acute delirium, substance dependence or withdrawal, depression, and anxiety. Occasionally, one of us would need to try to bring some order back to one of the medical wards, after havoc was wreaked by an out-of-control borderline patient. A borderline patient in crisis on the medical ward are to their staff as a heart attack would be to a psychiatric units' staff. Professor Maltbie once lectured about the borderline patient in crisis as analogous to baby birds, mouths wide open, appetite insatiable, and helpless to find food for themselves, so they just sit in the nest and wait for the mother to bring them precious delicacies (worms) all day long. They never are satisfied or quiet unless they are in the act of feeding. The emotional needs of a borderline patient are equivalent to the appetites of those baby hatchlings. The emotional needs of a patient with borderline personality in acute crisis are never met to their satisfaction. The patient must be placated until discharged. Transfer to Psych is usually not desired because the Psych unit usually does not need any extra problems either, since chances are that a nest of baby birds already reside there, and you don't want to make any more enemies with staff than absolutely necessary.

A rare case of Munchausen's has been known to present. This is a disease where the patient has a psychological and pathological need to be medically ill. Therefore, the patient will go to unbelievable lengths to meet criteria for admission to the hospital. The case I recall involved a woman who had multiple hospitalizations across the country. Of course, she did not provide this information. Finding the information, however, broke the case, causing her to leave in anger for the next hospital. These very sick puppies routinely go as far as injecting feces into their wounds. Even worse, a variation of the disorder known as Munchausen's by proxy involves the parent inflicting injury or infection on their own child, in order to keep the children constantly hospitalized. Such cases are usually found exclusively at University or tertiary care centers.

PGY-3 included six months of child psychiatry. Working with the kids was not a problem, but dealing with the parents and the school system was not guaranteed to go smoothly. Overall, it was not a bad experience. At the University setting, evaluations were usually quite tedious and as comprehensive as possible. The process was a little too multi-disciplinary for one such as me who likes autonomy and independence. Although it was not the subspecialty for me, I still ended up having to treat many kids, due to the lack of child psychiatrists in the community. Actually, treating children and adolescents in the family setting has turned out to be challenging and rewarding. Those six months of training turned out to be a very practical investment of time.

I would estimate that about 75% of child psychiatry cases in general practice involve one or more of just a few disorders. These are Attention Deficit Hyperactivity Disorder, Oppositional Defiant Disorder, Conduct Disorder, Developmental Disorders (congenital or acquired from maternal substance abuse), Autistic Disorders, Bipolar Disorder, and Learning Disorders including Dyslexia and Central Auditory Processing Disorder. Blend in a couple of psychosocial problems, such as domestic violence, poverty, no father or alcoholism in the home, and you get a kid with major issues.

The incidence of incest and childhood sexual, emotional, and physical abuse, reported and unreported cases discovered years later, in my opinion, would surpass the whole abortion issue politically in no time flat. However, no politician wishes to touch the issue because he may find out he has to do something about it. The abortion issue has many years of political mileage before it is finally acknowledged publicly that no decision but pro-choice is compatible with the majority of American society. Morality cannot be legislated. It also is a choice. Like many other social issues, the reality of incest and child abuse, which occurs with alarming regularity across all racial and socioeconomic boundaries, is quietly swept under the rug with several other issues equal to or more germane to our society than the abortion issue.

Treatments for some childhood psychiatric conditions such as the most frequently diagnosed ADHD are safe, effective, and able to make an enormous difference in the lives of many otherwise marginally functional or sub functional children. Some parents do not want their children to take medications, usually due to fear or ignorance, and everybody involved endures unnecessary distress. The drugs are safe enough in most cases that *the risks of a child going untreated are significantly greater* than using a stimulant to treat that child's condition. Behavior associated with ADHD exposes the child to increased risk from physical injury due to the tendency for impulsive and risky choices at home and on the playground. The child is more likely to become involved in fights. Self-esteem is damaged from inability to focus, sit still, and pay attention in class, which leads to suboptimal academic performance and ridicule from peers. The child may grow to dislike school placing him at higher risk for truancy, somatic complaints, and dropping out. Most untreated teens are tempted to self medicate, usually with cocaine, alcohol and marijuana as drugs of choice. By this point, the young adult may not be salvageable, and it will be just a matter of time before they become permanently a part of the criminal justice system. All this facilitated by the parents' choice not to trust the psychiatrist. To me, that in itself is neglectful and considered child abuse.

If action is not taken against some of the irresponsible law firms with open access to the media, soon a few cases of adverse reaction to a stimulant having no statistically significant meaning regarding safety of the medication will be leashed on the public. This campaign will be designed to excite fear, and ultimately could lead to mass hysteria and discontinuation of safe and effective medications. Should this occur, the result would be millions of untreated kids. This has already occurred successfully with several products, including the antidepressant Serzone, the multi-use product Neurontin (FDA approved to safely treat seizures), the antipsychotic and mood stabilizer Zyprexa, and to a lesser degree, SSRI antidepressants such as Prozac, Zoloft, and Paxil. Though millions have greatly benefited, unfortunately a few patients may have suffered severe adverse reactions. The real truth is that over the counter pain medications and other products have proven to be greatly more dangerous and have probably resulted in more fatalities than all of the above mentioned medications combined. As usual, the real motive here is money, of which the pharmaceutical companies undoubtedly have plenty. A sharp attorney can elicit a good settlement for his few clients and of course himself by just threatening to use the media. The media has no effective means of regulating this misinterpretation of scientific data, and usually promotes all or nothing thinking to those unable to comprehend that they or their loved one is in no more danger by continuing the medication than being struck by lightening the next time they walk out the door. It is in all probability that the patient will much more likely be killed driving to work or to commit suicide than to have a fatal reaction from a prescribed psychotropic medication. The subliminal attackers of SSRI antidepressants through the media actually have used this to their advantage, and have the built in advantage of 100% of its subjects diagnosed with a depressive illness. *The rate of suicide is multiple times greater among depressed individuals than the general population.* Qualified professionals always diagnose and treat depression. A few suicidal deaths are inherently going to occur no matter what the provider does. These professional providers are becoming the primary targets for future lawsuits. This is especially true with the FDA and the pharmaceutical companies now covering their behinds with a written disclaimer. If the trend of manipulation and exploitation does expand to include the stimulant medications, which probably have the greatest positive response to safety ratio than any class of drug with major use in psychiatry, it seems there will be one beneficiary in addition to the law firms.

Eli Lilly now makes a non-stimulant medication, Strattera, which looks promising as an alternative to stimulants. Strattera has demonstrated itself comparable to the stimulants in efficacy but does have the disadvantage of requiring several weeks to take effect.

The literature at this time supports a lower risk of future substance abuse among those treated with stimulants than those with untreated ADHD. The argument that the use of stimulants leads to future substance abuse is unfounded scientifically. Statistics estimate up to 80% of adults with ADHD go undiagnosed and untreated.

❧

PGY-4, like fourth year medical school, is a time to take electives and look forward to the future. I chose to do Student Health, Forensic Psychiatry, Correctional Psychiatry, HMO Psychiatry, and a day of AHEC at the Blue Ridge Center in Asheville, NC. The airplane was all mine this time. This was the year to begin terminating therapy with patients and helping them get set up with another provider. I felt sad about some of them, but the future excitement outweighed that. I found that this year wasn't that exciting, although working with inmates at the Wake County Jail and Mental Health Center was interesting. Most amazing was to discover that everyone in the jail had been framed, or was a victim of mistaken identity. That's some conspiracy! It's almost always a game with that crew. Ninety percent of assessing the inmates is reading between the lines and finding out what they really want. Code words are *nerves bad, Xanax, can't take anti-depressants, got the shakes, you can call my doctor, my back is killing me, migraines, starts with an X, klonopins, valiums, vicoden, percocets, ain't slept in days.* Once any of those words are heard, it's predictable where the interview is headed.

I used Klonopin (a controlled drug for treating anxiety and agitation) when I felt it to be appropriate in the jail setting, as opposed to some doctors who choose *never* to use benzodiazepines or opioid pain medications. This assures no substance abuse, at least until they can get it somewhere else. It also assures that honest, non-abusing patients suffer more than is necessary. The honest to God truth is that drug abusers are going to abuse drugs until they decide to stop, or until they die, because abusing drugs is what drug abusers do, period. Whether you prescribe to them or not, they will abuse at the first opportunity. I would rather treat them in a controlled manner than worry about them breaking into my home one night. I think it's better to treat all patients the way your training dictates and those who sincerely want to be helped by your treatment will receive its benefits. Those who receive by deceit and lies will continue to get what they deserve. The joke is on them. Occasionally, one of those abusers may actually benefit from the treatment received and they will stop abusing substances or taking their medications inappropriately. The doctor should do his or her job and not try to fix the world. If the *first do no harm* commitment remains intact, the doctor has done no wrong ethically and has helped the maximum number of patients within his or her power.

I chose to elaborate on this topic because it is so problematic and the problem will get worse as long as the system continues to criminalize and warehouse chemically dependent people without providing effective treatment of their core problems.

As the year progressed, I started to look around for where to begin my career. I sent out a few letters and waited for responses. I knew that I wanted to remain in the Piedmont region, so I interviewed for a position at Charter Hospital in Raleigh and talked to a couple of psychiatrists in Greensboro. I wasn't really enthused about either. One of my colleagues informed me of the mental health center where she was starting a job and said they were still looking for doctors. Burlington was an excellent location and starting to develop into a nice area to settle. I went on an interview, which went well, and let them know I was interested. Next came the hard part.

My life had been on hold for so long, from a financial and social standpoint, that there was some excitement about the future. Mortgage companies and other financial institutions were throwing credit at me, without even having to ask. This was weird, considering all the loans I had been denied over the past years. I could barely get a loan officer to talk to me before. All of a sudden, I could have basically whatever I asked for.

During the last six months of 1996, my life changed enormously. In the first week of July, the training wheels came off and, for the first time, I was making treatment decisions without having to answer to an attending. There was no longer a built-in safety to second-guess or provide an additional opinion. This took some getting used to. Now, once the order was written, unless it was something obviously inappropriate, it was carried out by nursing.

Away from the university, a doctor still enjoyed significant prestige and respect. It was almost like being royalty, the way I was catered to. It tended to make me uncomfortable at times, because in my experience, when people treated you so nicely and respectfully, either you were about to be hit up for a large amount of money or lured into a deadly trap. I finally got use to the brown-nosing and realized it was just a formality. Behind closed doors, the doctor was the subject of gossip, just like everyone else.

Some say mental health center work is difficult, but after residency training it was hard to believe that I was actually getting paid for what I was doing. That is probably how I eventually started to do so much extra work. *Hard* is the only way I know when it comes to work. There is no better place to gain work experience than the mental health center, since there the most difficult patients are usually treated.

I purchased a home that July, accepting the reality of my days as a bachelor coming to a rapid halt. I felt like it was time to settle down. My fiancé, Pia, whom I had met at Dorothea Dix, where she worked as an R.N., had no problem arranging a wedding in our home for December 31st. She was also an evangelist in the Pentecostal Church, which made living in sin a very unattractive option. In just a matter of months, I had become responsible for the treatment of hundreds of patients, bought a home, and taken on a wife and 13-year-old stepdaughter. Naturally, mowing the grass, gardening, and landscaping became my new favorite activities. I also became educated about plants and flowers.

Gardening helped take me back to childhood, when I collected worms behind Johnny's tractor and when I looked forward to planting my own little garden. My new home was located next to a pond, so I could fish whenever I wanted to. Today, more than anything, I regret having not taken more time to enjoy my home. I understand the saying that no one on their deathbed ever commented about wishing they had spent more time at the office.

During 1998, my cousin Lewis died of cancer at age fifty-seven, just as Uncle Johnny had. Later that year, my brother, Earl, died from leukemia and we had a chance to put the past behind us. It turned out that he comforted me during his last hours, when I had to let go of my denial that a remission in the leukemia had occurred. I wrote his obituary, realizing how short this life really is. I had brothers who died at ages twenty-seven, thirty-seven, and forty-two. My cousin, Mike, was killed in a car accident a few years prior to this writing. Most of my aunts and uncles have gone on, or will be going in the near future. This is a part of the evolution of the universe. Souls come and souls go. We cry for those who die and worry about those who may die. I believe that those who have retuned to God should probably cry for us survivors on earth.

Encountering death on a frequent basis, with the grief work, has helped me to grow spiritually. A universal truth is that the deceased loved one would never want the survivor to spend their precious time worrying and crying over them. In reality, it will be a finite amount of time before that survivor joins them.

However, the grieving process must occur for healing to occur. One should never resist the process described by Dr. Kuebler-Ross, involving shock, denial, anger, guilt, depression/despair, and finally acceptance and the state of being healed.

In September 2001, I left the mental health center to give my own thing a shot. On TV, I watched the second plane crash into the trade center on the Tuesday morning before I officially started. I suppose it was a part of my fate for me to start at that time, since more people than usual would be requiring appointments. Finding patients has not been a problem, due to a shortage in providers. At this point, job security is not an issue.

I'm fortunate to not be a part of the public mental health delivery system at the current time because of its very uncertain future. Even though, I still feel much compassion for the patients involved with reform of the system. Unfortunately, they sometimes seem to be of least importance based on many of the political decisions made and what, at this time, appears to be poorly thought out planning. Thus far, many of the sickest patients from Dorothea Dix are flooding the County Jail where I work eight hours a week. There is no psychiatric staff at the jail. The neglect some of these patients unfairly receive really makes me angry sometimes. Yet I feel helpless to do anything about the situation, other than write in my AOL Journal. I understand these patients better than anyone involved with them, including themselves. Yet, the process involving the course of their future treatment takes place with politicians behind closed doors and excludes me from participating in any meaningful way. To put my faith in those I have no reason to trust to do the right thing, I am at this time required to do. I suppose this is my opportunity to understand what a patient feels inside when I ask them to put their trust in me.

CHAPTER 27

Spirituality

The Soul Endures Forever, Regardless

On May 12, 2001, my life changed. It was a Saturday no different from any other beautiful spring day, bright and sunny. I left Chapel Hill around 3:15 p.m. and headed down Interstate Highway 85 South, destination High Point, N.C. Crossing the bridge over the Haw River, I remember how picturesque the water appeared. There seemed to be something special and calming about this day. Then, almost out of nowhere, a dark cloud appeared and it began to rain. It then began to pour down. I slowed down the '98 Pathfinder. Driving in the rain had never been a big deal.

Almost as suddenly as it started, the downpour let up. I continued to drive on, with Smokey Robinson playing loudly in the CD player. The road was very wet, but visibility was fine. With twenty-seven years of driving experience, operating a vehicle was a lot like walking, in that little voluntary thought was required. I have done some of my best thinking while driving down the open highway. This particular afternoon was no different from a hundred others, or so I thought. My vehicle was in the second lane from the shoulder, which is where the slower traffic usually is. An eighteen-wheeler surprised me by passing in the right lane and drenching my vehicle. My reflex reaction was to check the lane to my left and change lanes immediately, which I did. While turning the steering wheel to the left, there was a sensation of the back of the vehicle rising from the pavement and moving to the right. This had happened once before in this vehicle, and I was able to recover, never giving it much thought. This time was different. The vehicle began to fishtail as I desperately fought the wheel. At this point, a surreal feeling took over, as if what was happening was not really happening. It couldn't be. In an instant, control of the vehicle and control of my life were no longer with me. I didn't know how this was going to end and I realized that it was no longer up to me. There was nothing more I could do. This was the moment of truth, where it was all to end.

The vehicle slid perpendicular to the cement median that divided the eight lanes and I wondered how much pain I was going to feel. Everything was occurring in slow motion. It became clear that I would crash into the three-foot plus high median. As impact was made, there was a sound like none I've heard before or since. It was a sound of metal crunching and glass exploding. The airbag activated with such force that my hands were blasted from the steering wheel. I watched the passenger side air bag inflate instantly, though Guardian would not require it. Guardian apparently entered as the voice of Smokey was extinguished.

All at once, there was quiet and I felt wind and raindrops against my face. I was expecting pain, so this sensation actually felt good. My endorphins had taken effect, causing the sensation of calm. By this time, I had resigned from resistance and was ready to accept my fate. The vehicle slid several feet before rolling over and coming to rest upside down.

A moment passed before I realized that I was still alive. I heard the voices of motorists running to help. I'm sure they were expecting to see a mutilated or dead body. I was sitting perfectly in the seat, except for being upside down, and I couldn't see anyone. A gentleman communicated with me through the crushed passenger side window. Another gentleman reached through my window to turn the ignition off. I heard a crowd gather. "He's okay," someone said. "Just shook up."

I suppose I figured that since they all had come to see me, I shouldn't let them down, so I unsnapped the seatbelt and fell to what was left of the roof. There was a small applause and gasps as I crawled out the driver's side window, showing no significant injuries. Guardian had come through again. I was actually more upset about the loss of my transportation than anything else. Someone offered me the kind gesture of a blanket, but I didn't need it.

Two state troopers arrived and began securing the situation. One of them told me how fortunate I was to walk away from such an accident. The ambulance was late, because there had actually been two other accidents at different locations. All I had to show the paramedic was a whelp on my wrist from the airbag. That was good, because I didn't want to go to the same hospital where I worked.

I was angry but still in a little shock. Erroneously, I told the trooper the vehicle had rolled over two or three times when it had rolled once. He rewarded me with a speeding ticket. The fact that I was alive caused me not to be upset. I returned to the vehicle to collect a few items, before the tow truck started to work. In the middle of the highway lay a book that had been ejected during the collision. It was about God. I thought about what a coincidence this was and a strange feeling came over me.

Using my cell phone, I called Pia, who picked me up at the towing station. I went home, took a hot bath, and then went to the hospital to see patients. The thought of why I was alive was implanted in my mind.

Since that day, my outlook on life has been different. The thought of that day reminds me that I could be dead. There is a reason I'm still here and I tend to search for that reason in everything I experience. My cousin, Walter, recently had what sounded like the same accident in his SUV and he was killed. Why am I still here and he's not? I do know that there are no accidents, that we're all on our own personal journey through this life. The choices we make determine how things are played out. We do have free will and a certain amount of control over the course of our life.

This accident let me experience the feeling of losing that free will and that control. For the time the vehicle was out of control, nothing was certain any longer about my life. During those moments, I understood who was really in control, that the only thing that belonged to me for that instance was the life I had already lived; a life that was incomplete. A life that had often been taken for granted and lived as though it would last indefinitely.

The free will we are blessed with should not be taken for granted. That is not what was intended. Our free will cannot be appreciated fully until we realize it can be taken away. For many, it is too late when that discovery is finally made. I was blessed with the chance to appreciate mine in a way many never will. If everyone had a near death experience, the world might be a better place.

I decided to take a break from traditional religion and explore some things for myself. I was having difficulty with a lot that was being taught, and with the Bible in general. I wanted to believe all, but some things were not adding up. I got into Books on Tape and, while driving to and from jobs, began listening to everything I could get my hands on. Out of everything I found, I treasure the work of Walsch, Chopra, and Zukav the most. These authors have broken it down in a way that I can understand and in a way that makes sense. Again, no matter what level of spirituality one reaches, the message is always simple and the same. Jesus put it best with the command to love the Lord thy God with all thy heart and soul and love your brother as yourself. By sincerely following this commandment, there is no way to go wrong, but it will only work when all involved play by the same rules. At this time, we are not at that point.

Have you ever wondered how it all began? Man has forever sought an answer to this question. I have grown to believe that the vast majority of information in the universe is too sophisticated for our minds to comprehend. Our minds are an excellent tool for navigating through this earthly experience. That is what our five senses and brains were created to do. I am beginning to believe that we have it all wrong. We do not go through life, but quite the opposite, life goes through us. For most people, the Holy Bible is all that they need for peace and consolation. Thank God for the Holy Bible because it serves its purpose well.

I do not expect anyone to agree with my beliefs, because the beauty of the whole thing is that we all have to seek truth for ourselves. We all are on a personal journey. When our time ends here, we move on into the unknowns of eternity. While here, some of us choose to consciously grow and some do not. One may choose to spend their years on earth as one chooses. As for me, I am driven to know as much as possible. There are so many things to know outside of our earthly realm that an attempt at really imagining this would probably lead to insanity.

Neale Donald Walsch, author of the Conversations With God series, has really influenced my way of thinking. His writings informed me that God is speaking to me as well as him, confirmed by the fact I was led to listen to it. The tape spoke of the limitations of words. Words are the least effective way to associate with God because words are another creation of man. God needs nothing as archaic as a word created by a human mind to communicate with us, yet we continue searching for God through our own creation of words and language. If we were to drop the words and listen to our intuition, we could be drawn even closer to each other and to the Maker.

Gary Zukav, of Seat of the Soul, illustrates beautifully the reality of evolution to come. This will involve gaining more access to that ninety percent of our mind and brain that we do not use. Once we learn to tap into that, we will develop into multi-sensory beings. Our societies will then begin to live up to full potential. Zukav goes on to make a case for our salvation lying in authentic power, which differs from man's current route of external power. The external realm tends to separate man from each other and from God. The physical realm is just one branch of the mother realm, which is the spirit. God can only be truly understood in the spiritual realm. A search for God in the physical realm is always unproductive. That mode results in overlooking God. So to speak, we don't see the forest for the trees because of our tendency to experience life through tunnel vision. Remember that material things, including our bodies and minds, are transient and designed to expire. One day, in the distant future, our sun will expand to scorch the earth as it begins to cool and approaches its own death. Our solar system will have lived out its life. The very life that runs through us today will be required to return to the Creator or redistributed about the eternal universe. Another super nova will explode with incomprehensible energy and force, spawning billions of new suns and planets, some of which will nurture and sustain life again, until the cycle repeats itself over billions of what were once known as human years.

Who or what will appreciate humankind after these events? Maybe it won't even matter what events occurred during the era of that little blue planet once known as earth. We can only wonder where our consciousnesses will be experiencing life in the greater and timeless reality. I have no trouble believing what I've just written, and it doesn't contradict any major religion. I processed this information to arrive at a concept that makes sense to me. Anyone who has come about their own beliefs by believing what someone else told them should not criticize or judge. Beliefs also should evolve as one accumulates additional information on the journey to truth. We haven't arrived anywhere near ultimate reality, but we are closer to it than we were five thousand years ago, at least in the physical realm. I believe discovery of ultimate reality will reveal how much greater our souls are when not confined to a human body. The afterlife should be more wonderful than our words can describe or our minds can imagine.

Dr. Deepak Chopra, author of several great books, is unbelievably brilliant. One must be at a certain spiritual level to even begin to accept and understand what he is saying. The three authors mentioned thus far provide different ways for looking at the same reality. They are not to be feared, because nothing they write contradicts that which is ultimately true. Many fundamentalists would refer to them as false prophets. I compare that to saying that the world is flat or there was a conspiracy to plant dinosaur bones.

The fear in many religions cripples the growth of their own members, by not providing an opportunity for them to explore the world of creative thought. This is effectively done through the threat of everlasting fire. This way of thinking was necessary thousands of years ago, because there was no way to get primitive man's attention, other than to threaten him with destruction. Mythology was state-of-the-art communication in earlier times.

Thank God for mythology. This is the reason so much emphasis has been placed on quality education. One route to reaching a higher level is through education. Through this route, man has to master words and language, which again are the most basic forms of communication with God. A large fund of information about man's environment is also essential. Once this fund of knowledge and mastery of communication have been obtained, man receives a document called a degree. Man can then realize the simplicity of the profound answers sought. The same answers man finds were coded in the mythology once thought to be primitive and elementary.

It always ends up going full circle, no matter where one begins. Actually, an illiterate person is capable of graduating to higher levels, but our society forces that person to believe they are not good enough, when in reality we all are equal at the soul level. What one will find repeatedly is that all roads ultimately lead to God, but that it is up to you to travel the road you find most compatible.

I am trying hard to avoid any plagiarism here, because there are certain concepts and references that are universally true, making it impossible not to duplicate some information. What is truth for one is truth for all, or it never was truth to start with. Different authors have different methods of revealing truth. When ideas match up so perfectly with other scribes, it confirms that the source is genuine. I know that authors of the truth have one goal, which is to spread that truth. The truth comes directly from God, as Mr. Walsch has so eloquently stated in his conversations with God.

Dr. Chopra helped influence me to write this book. His message agrees with Mr. Walsch's, stating the importance of believing that you are already where you strive to be. Due to physical laws, time cannot be omitted. Belief will draw what you desire to you. I am testing his hypothesis, because I see myself as a successfully published author of a popular book. I have the confidence to write this book in that way and allow fate to do the rest.

Mr. Zukav taught me to think in a multi-sensory manner and follow my intuition. That intuition tells me that God wants more out of me and that He, as always, will prepare a way for this to happen. I have faith that the proper people and proper situations will appear at the proper time, as the story of my life thus far has demonstrated.

There are readers who feel uncomfortable with peering outside their own beliefs. This is totally fear-based and is triggered by the thought of going to hell. I no longer fear going to hell, though you may think I will "bust it wide open." If one can get past that thought, there is another whole universe outside. God does not want us to fear Him. All He really wants is for us to let His/Her love flow through us and touch others. Simply, that is the essence of the human experience on earth. It allows us to experience what does not exist in the heavenly realm. Concepts such as pain, depression, suffering, misery, hatred, and jealousy may not exist in the heavenly realm. Without evil, good cannot exist. Without sadness, there can be no happiness. Without grief, there can be no rejoicing.

Author Gary Zukav uses a brilliant analogy for comparing man to God, stating that upon birth the soul of man is like dipping a cup of water from the ocean. At death, that cup of water is returned to the ocean. The cup represents the human body, the ocean represents God. The question is whether the water that was in the cup still exists when put back into the ocean. Will your life exist upon leaving the body and when your soul returns to the eternal ocean of God?

Think of the Bible passage that states that man was created in the image of God. Our souls are micro-images of God.

There is only one life and that life is the very essence of what God is. That life flows through every creature on earth and through countless creatures on other planets throughout the universe.

This is where some readers begin to say to themselves that I have lost my natural born mind. Twenty years ago, I would have also called this nonsense. However, twenty years ago I was also much more ignorant than I am today. If I am alive twenty years from today, I will state the same about being more ignorant today. Our awareness never ceases to evolve, it just evolves at the rate we allow it to evolve. Therefore, in the past twenty years, I have stopped letting myself be controlled by fear, at least from a spiritual standpoint. That fear brought me to where I am, and I am grateful. I do not require that fear-based theology in my life any longer. Moreover, if you think I am going to hell, I do not care. You may not make it to heaven yourself, because of your judgmental tendencies.

I am developing my own personal relationship with God. The beauty of true spirituality is that the infant, as well as the Alzheimer's sufferer understand it equally. No words are required. Fundamentally, there is heaven versus hell and good verses evil. Any fool can understand this concept, and if this works for you, use it. The truth is that the universe is not that simple. There are endless levels of spirituality and we all are free to expand to a higher level. We can advance until we reach heaven, if it were possible to go to heaven in a body. So far, Jesus Christ has been the only one reported to have accomplished that feat.

I see the heaven and hell fundamental as being analogous to behavioral therapy, such as behavior modification. At some point, one finally gets it and no longer needs the threat of eternal banishment to hell. At this point, the person does the right thing simply because it is the right thing to do. The person has graduated to a higher level. The person does not receive God's condemnation for taking it upon him or herself to participate in individual self-growth.

I believe that God is pleased for his spiritual offspring because they are making this effort to be more like the Maker. That is where we originated. I believe that one cannot avoid returning to God, in the words of Mr. Walsch. Anyone thinking in this manner opens the door to becoming a true leader and an ambassador of God's love.

My favorite word in the English language is *infinity*. I love the word because, within infinity, the answers to all questions lie. Infinity cannot be comprehended by our earthly minds, yet we know almost for certain that it is a reality. The idea of infinity suggests that whatever every human that ever lives can imagine in their mind already exists somewhere in the universe, though probably outside the range of human comprehension. That is another way of saying that anything is possible. Using our logic, none of this makes sense. Maybe it is true that our existence is really the dream, and ultimate reality lies somewhere in the virtual or dream world.

We all have a date scheduled with death, and it is at that time that we will finally know. The Big Bang theory suggests that an inconceivable amount of energy exploded from an infinitely small singularity. Some of this energy became matter. One law of physics states that matter can be neither created nor destroyed, but can only be reconverted back to energy. Different atomic combinations developed the elements. Carbon atoms became the essential ingredient for developing the components that support life on earth. The scientific community has good evidence for backing these claims.

The state of existence that no human can conceive, and perhaps never will, is what happened before the Big Bang? There is not a single clue. This is why faith is essential. Before the Big Bang, Creation, or whatever words you select, there was no need for religion or science. Neither can be traced before that point. Religion and science started together, and in the end, they will end together. The two are not mutually exclusive.

In fact, the two compliment each other, as do mind, body, and soul. One author put it well when he illustrated God as being the hub of a bicycle wheel with all of creation leading back, like the infinite spokes.

CHAPTER 28

The Goal of Self Actualization

The Real Key to It All

The state of self-actualization is probably the highest state one can reach in this life. I have not yet reached that state, but I believe I have found the path. If I live long enough, I will reach it one day. When this state is reached, the soul is at peace. It is a place of truth, where the mystics and sages lounge. In this state, one transcends the petty concerns of life.

The first step involves gaining control of more than a single point of perspective. A good therapist is capable of transforming their perspective into that of a fly on the wall. From this perspective, the phenomenon of transference becomes much clearer. The therapist can read how the patient is reacting and simultaneously maintain his or her own feelings of counter-transference. . For example, a female patient may transfer fatherly love or hatred onto her male therapist, causing the therapist to experience feelings of wanting to comfort her...or wanting the session to end as soon as possible. The therapist is in the unique position of being able to freeze that moment in time for closer analysis. When this particular patient behaves in the exact same manner with a man who is not in a therapeutic environment, but in the real world, that man will respond to his counter-transference feeling in a manner that she is pleased with or finds disturbing. This exact dynamic may be the source of what has led the person to therapy in the first place. She may have grown up without a father, which may have arrested her in an emotional state where she desires fatherly advice, or where she desires to feel like she belongs to a father. With every man she comes in contact, she sends out this transference, which may be totally innocent. Nevertheless, 99% of the men she comes in contact with are not psychotherapists and don't necessarily have her ultimate well-being at heart. A well-seasoned predator (player) will be skilled at picking up on this transference and exploiting the young lady to his own advantage. He will tell her exactly what she wants to hear. He will make her feel like a beloved daughter and give her insincere fatherly advice. Her transference will then develop into an erotic transference, leading to lapses in judgment and her feelings of being in love. This is where the danger zone begins. She is most vulnerable at this point. Had she already been in therapy for a while, she might be aware of the dynamic that is unfolding. She might remember her pattern of pain caused by failed relationships, because of falling for the wrong type guy. She would see the warning signs and know that pain and disappointment lie ahead.

Suppose the man is not a predator, but a well-adjusted person with the best of intentions. In this case, her transference pattern may not be a liability, but may actually facilitate the initiation of a healthy or benign relationship.

Another possibility is role reversal, where the guy craves motherly love and treats the females he comes in contact with as if they were his mother. He could be the man of every woman's dreams, but if the woman he meets hates men from a pattern of being hurt her, he is in big trouble. His transference to her could be to protect her, or have her take care of him, depending on what his actual experience was with his own mother.

These hypothetical situations are actually played out each day across the country. The patient finally comes for therapy when he or she gets tired of repeatedly being hurt and not understanding why. Most patients are not aware of the larger dynamic occurring, or exactly how their own behavior contributes to the same results over and over. A seasoned therapist has experienced certain behaviors from patients many times, making them aware that people are more alike than they are different. As mentioned before, the therapist can use himself or herself as the object of the patient's transference, which automatically triggers a counter-transference upon which the therapist knows not to act. The therapist can pretty accurately assume that if the patient's transference evokes a particular reaction from them, it is very probable that others experience the same counter-transference feelings when interacting with the patient in the real world.

The goal of the therapist becomes to direct the patient's attention to the behavior that evokes the response from others that leads them down the pathway to unhappiness. Most patients will resist an interpretation at this time because the denial must be broken down. The therapist must make a judgment as to whether or not the patient is capable of receiving insight into how their own behavior plays the leading role in their unhappiness. Many patients will have already developed a defense of blaming others and will never see their own behavior as suspect. Patients with the opposite personality would feel so much guilt that they would take the blame for everything wrong in the relationship, as well as their responsibility for every bad thing that ever happened to every person in their life. One behavior is equally as bad as the other.

The above situations are common examples of the types of neuroses that cause many relationships to suffer and fail. This also illustrates the value of a good insight-oriented psychotherapist who has total trust of the patient. I chose to use insight-oriented psychotherapy as an example of what type of growth is required for a person to be capable of reaching the state of self-actualization. That person must be able to see what psychological scars and flaws they still possess from encounters with toxic people during their developmental years. That person must then be able to understand how they defend psychologically against these flaws. Two of the more common defenses are mentioned above in the manner of *blame and denial* (externalization), or *guilt* and *over-acceptance* (internalization). Both are effective defenses, but are neurotic and mentally unhealthy.

The desired outcome is for the person to go through the process of gaining that insight of why they behave the way they do. Next, the person will strive to learn healthier coping mechanisms, in which they are in control, as opposed to being controlled by a learned behavior that no longer serves a positive purpose or, even worse, serves a harmful purpose. When a person reaches that point, they can enter the path to self-actualization. The psychological and emotional bonds to the negativity can then be transcended through the pathway of truth.

The next goal is to merge this revived mind with a spiritual life that is healthy. This creates a shield against any stressor this world can offer. You realize you are living *in* this world, but you are not *of* this world. There is no longer a fear of death. Since practically all diseases arise from the effects of external stress, the body eventually can theoretically regain its natural healing powers and, in addition, can begin to reverse any inherited gene mutation for future generations to perpetuate. This, of course, is a simplistic and superficial model, but I believe the theory could fly.

I recommend that one begin self-examination of daily transference/counter-transference reactions to get an estimate of the baggage picked up from living life. Many times, when I was into the Internet, I found myself fuming over some comment someone may have sent me. I have also felt my self-esteem boosted from some typed comment. Any reader preoccupied with the question of why I was on the internet should stop reading now, because you won't get this: a certain degree of objectivity is required for an understanding. If you were focused on the why, you are probably a subjective, judgmental, externalizer. Also, you'll be clueless about those descriptions, so just skip the rest of this chapter.

Any reader feeling insulted at this point is experiencing an inferiority complex.

The harshness of these words is intentional and purposeful. What you are feeling was totally created in your own mind and is only real to you; the rest of the universe is not the least bit concerned. You allowed a few words on a piece of paper to determine how and what you feel. This probably happens to you hundreds of times each day. You allow your emotions to lead you, which cause you to be worried, irritable, angry, guilty, or depressed. There's not much room left for happiness or joy. Those not affected by the above trap, are more likely to be in a good state of mental health.

My original point about the Internet involved me sitting in front of a machine. Not a real person, but a man-made machine. While sitting there reading words from some semi-anonymous person in another time zone, I found myself going through the full range of emotion.

Question: Does a machine have the power to inject emotions into a man who is believed to be intelligent? I think not. You might say that it's not really the machine doing it, that there's a human source.

Question: Would it really matter if it were a person at the other end or a robot or another computer? The fact is that a person normally thought to be in his right mind is sitting there interacting with some metal and plastic chips and feeling human emotions. Everything this person is feeling is actually being manufactured in his mind. In other words, it's a total fantasy. Some may disagree, but this is where free will and choice enter the equation. Fantasies are voluntary or chosen, not inflicted upon another. Fantasies are only a problem when the fantasizer believes they are real. More clearly, what is really happening is that the person is triggering the subconscious to release stored emotion from past times. What the person is feeling may have happened ten years ago. The mind doesn't know ten years ago from ten minutes ago, unless the operator of the mind tells it so. Enthralled in fantasyland, the operator isn't telling the mind anything. The owner/operator of this poor brain is allowing it to run down the freeway, with no one at the wheel. The person may be feeling what he felt during the last time he reached out to another and was made to feel welcome and loved or rejected and despised.

If those emotions were never properly dealt with, trust me, they are coming back for more. That is why it's recommended to grieve the loss of an ended relationship before even considering a serious new relationship. Many make the mistake of repeatedly falling in love impulsively and stacking up the baggage. With all this baggage, a healthy relationship is impossible. The person then forces away one partner after another, or continues in a dysfunctional relationship and develops severe emotional problems or chemical dependency.

The woman who repeatedly allows her spouse to abuse her is deeply asleep at the wheel and a plethora of negativity eats at her mind, soul and, eventually, her body. The answers are hard, but fair: Stop letting your past run your present. Clean out your closet. Find a good therapist and dump some of that baggage.

The negative feelings that were swept under the rug or thrown into the closet, are demons returning from the past. You thought they were gone or that it was over, but those demons are there every day and will haunt you until the day you die, unless you choose to try a different path than the current one.

The mistake many people make is getting about a dollar's worth of religion and believing that God is going to cure them of what problems they face. These people immediately begin to judge, denouncing such disciplines as psychology and psychiatry, the very place God has sent them to help themselves. Usually these people already believe they know everything they need to know. They must be allowed time to fall flat on their face, which is guaranteed to happen.

God gave us this world and this life to fulfill the potentials He planted in us. Some have hard lives, while others seem to have it made. Despite the life one has lived on earth, at the end we must return to the place of our origin. I find it pointless to make any effort to clarify this state of being, for the truth is that no human knows, nor can any human imagine. I do hold the belief that some way we will return to our maker and thank Him for allowing us to experience what we interpreted as misery. At that moment, we will realize that it was never as bad as we made it out to be.

Another definition of *crazy* is chaos or lacking order. Physics uses a principal or law known as entropy to extract order from disorder. Sigmund Freud and other analysts used a term known as free association to extract an understanding from the chaos and confusion of a neurotic patient's thoughts. Such a process sometimes took years for progress to occur. We all have access to meditation and can customize a means of it that is suitable, if the willingness to feel a little awkward and crazy is there. Meditation, I have heard is good for the soul. There are different means of meditation. For me, writing has been most effective. I don't believe there is a correct or incorrect method. This chapter shall be concluded with a written meditation that came to be through spontaneity of thought.

You of us, once I, anticipates the reality of a future of glorious bliss and incomprehensible Nirvana. A reality exponentially of greater magnificent than humanly imaginable, re-birthed from memories of earthly life so brief the insignificance of time again becomes clear. Recall human consciousness that existed in the dimension of time, no longer having relevance. Emotions now rendered neutral and meaningless for the glorious bliss trumps all. Earthly ultra-low frequencies have nearly faded, replaced by infinite frequencies of light energy caressing and bathing the point you of us chooses to be until choosing to be no longer. Imagine the weightlessness of a body without mass and not governed by Newton's physics or even Einstein's relativity, but by thought and perfect intelligence independent of gray matter, neurotransmitters and myelin sheaths. Size so small it rides comfortably within or upon the simplest thought and fits infinite times inside the enormous nucleus of an atom of hydrogen of a water molecule that once flowed through the physical vessel of you of us before returning to the sea seen as mighty during that existence, yet now clearly seems even smaller than possible, yet somehow the size is greater than nine trillion universes or more The shear fabric of the universe conducts the divine configuration of celestial energy that became the you of us when I chose to divide infinitely to create a duality and the genesis of the grandest of all self-awareness. Here there are no beginnings or endings unless our choice is to create them, just as mankind of earth was created from earth to perpetuate even more creating, as humans there still create from moment to moment with random thoughts they accept and reject in accordance with the thoughtless choices they often make. They pray to our self, looking for answers they already possess eternal access to, and waste the most precious gift of time rewarding the pleasure centers of their own brains, forgetting the us of you, the eternal origin of glorious bliss. In the virtual world, there is only one brain and one human, which divides and multiplies infinitely and may never choose to be one again until called home with the final expiration of the era, nor did the heart and soul of man, which is the you of us. As a human, the you of us did not realized the physical body was never who you really were but was merely a vehicle for practical purposes as this expiration has revealed, as the you of us is reborn into this eternal home that is without limits or boundaries of physical dimensions and the hindrance of time that brought you to again know equal and countless dimensions, now welcoming the return of you of us back to YOU of ME.

If you can make any sense of this writing, you can master chaos and disorder. It basically is an exercise of balancing left brain with right brain. Within infinity and eternity, all answers exist and there has never been a need for the concept humans have come to know as *impossible*. Our finite minds are everything to us at the present point along our cosmic journey, but in ultimate reality, a.k.a. The Big Scheme of Things, our minds are a micro-creation designed for a micro-purpose known to us as life on earth. Perceiving ones existence on this scale helps remove some of the narcissism from the thought, with an ultimate purpose of creating a state of consciousness conducive to meditating.

CHAPTER 29

A Day in the Life of the Author

(Disclaimer: All patients mentioned in this chapter are fictional)

If there is one thing that makes my job interesting, it is that no two days are exactly alike. Without this important distinguishing factor, the work could become intolerable. In the field of psychiatry, the doctor can create his own niche of the type of practice desired. A few of the options are adult psychiatry, child and adolescent psychiatry, geri-psychiatry, forensic psychiatry, inpatient psychiatry, outpatient psychiatry, community psychiatry, chemical dependency, public practice, private practice, group practice, consult liaison psychiatry, psychodynamic insight oriented psychiatry, psychoanalysis, dialectic behavioral therapy, psychopharmacology, emergency psychiatry, electroconvulsive therapy, cognitive behavioral therapy, hypnosis, minority psychiatry, correctional psychiatry. There are many other areas of subspecialty, but these give an idea of the range of opportunities for developing a practice.

There has never been a more exciting time to practice, and the profession has never enjoyed such credibility, prestige, and acceptance from other health care professionals. On the other hand, there has never been a more frustrating time to be involved with the uncertainties of how the delivery system will be dismantled and reconstituted. At the time of this writing, I see very little to be optimistic about, in regards to where things are headed. I hope that I am wrong.

The overall theme of the change is removing government responsibility and, ultimately, financial responsibility in the public sector of the mental health care delivery system. I could be misinformed, but it seems that many citizens requiring specialized care will be left to fend for themselves. Many will end up warehoused in jails and prisons, along with the addicts already there, making rich corporations richer and increasing the demand for more prisons to be built. Accomplishing this will be easy, since those who will be oppressed are those with the least power and status in society.

In the private sector, managed care companies and pharmaceutical companies will increasingly drain the insurance policies of hard working Americans. At the same time, the company CEO's will become billionaires. Left-over capital will be used to allow patients to have a few days of hospitalization every now and then, and even four or five sessions of outpatient treatment each year. Whoopee!

What more should these patients want? My personal sentiment is "to hell with managed care." Even if doctors kept their patients hospitalized a couple more days than they would be kept with managed care, the health care delivery system would still have enough capital left to treat millions of additional patients. I feel that subscribers to policies should be able to have their premiums invested into index market funds and benefit from the free market, instead of paying a third party to deny them of the care recommended by their physicians. Unfortunately, many of the politicians these very people vote for support managed care corporations efforts to pay out as few claim dollars as possible. The more care denied means the more profitable the corporation, meaning nobody looks out for the consumer.

Doctors rarely get involved because most of us went to medical school to learn how to treat disease, not to lobby for political changes. The best political and business minds seem to have left the medical profession, making it easier for third parties to have free reign on a major piece of the gross national product, while devoted physicians spend their time with excessive administrative paperwork. This assures that there will be no extra time for involvement with third party affairs. Numerous medical specialists have actually taken cuts in income.

I could be wrong, but I think something is not right about the CEO of any managed care company making ten times the annual income of the highest paid doctor on the panel. Can you place a monetary worth on your surgeon when you need a new heart or new liver? Would you want an overworked, underpaid, and unhappy pediatrician treating your child's meningitis? Would you even want to talk to a psychiatrist who's distracted by the anger she feels toward the case reviewer she just talked to on the phone and who overruled the request for three more days of hospitalization for a patient thinking of suicide? Who is worth more to you, your doctor or the artist blasting music into your teenager's ears through the earphones of his MP3 player? Your doctor cleared $150,000 before taxes last year; your son's musical artist collects that much in royalties each month from his last album. The guys warming the bench for your city's football team made twice as much money as your doctor did last year. Still, doctors are often criticized for making too much money. Fortunately, integrity and principal remain most important to those who care for the sick, along with many different dedicated professionals, such as those who teach your children. What would it be like if all the undervalued professionals in society decided to quit one day? That won't happen, because those who chose such professions didn't do so primarily to make money. Most of them were probably adequately gifted to have chosen more lucrative careers, if that had been their main desire.

Some may have been qualified to become the CEO of a managed care company, since that's where the real money seems to be.

I chose to spend so much time on my thoughts about managed care because interacting with those companies seems to irritate me the most, out of all the unpleasantness associated with practicing psychiatry. Second on that list of annoyances are policies and documentation policies, but these are at least viable and necessary evils. Overly needy patients, non-compliant patients, and drug addicts make my life miserable at times. On call days, another necessary evil can at times make you question your own sanity. The real American dream starts with being your own boss. For me, being able to sleep later is the prime benefit: I'm a late evening person and not at all a morning person. My biggest flaw is poor punctuality, followed by an inability to stick consistently to a schedule. I've made efforts to fix these flaws and have concluded that they aren't flaws, but traits that are a part of who I am and around which my work will have to be organized. Sometimes this is problematic, because it can be so out of sync with others. And sometimes conflict arises.

My days usually begin with a beep or a phone call about one of my inpatients or a consult. I listen to the Tom Joyner Show for a few laughs, then off to the shower to perform my Al Green impersonation. I take pleasure in not answering the phone until I get out of the shower and am good and ready to talk. I return the calls and handle the business. As I try to finish dressing, the beeper goes off. I finish dressing and systematically clip on my cell phone and beeper, place my checkbook wallet in my pocket, place my PDA and pens in my shirt pocket, clip on my badge, turn off all the lights, and head out the door. I return the beep, finding its Stacey in Medical Records telling me there are twelve charts to be completed by noon...or I'm facing a $100 fine and suspension of admitting privileges. Damn. "I was just in there three days ago," I tell him. "I'll be by in a few minutes, please have the charts ready."

Five seconds after hanging up the phone, the cuckoo chimes on my cell phone ring again. This time its Residential Treatment Services telling me they have two detox admissions from the Mental Health Center needing a physical examination. "Okay, I'll be by when I get a chance." As I approach the hospital, the phone rings again. It's the office, telling me to remember the review session with the managed care doctor at noon, and that there's a consult in the Critical Care Unit for an overdose. Shit. "I forgot I was on call today."

As I pull into the parking lot, the cuckoo rings again. It's the intake nurse. She's calling from the Emergency Room about an elderly patient who keeps wandering away from the rest home. He just lost his wife and was overheard saying that he wanted to jump off a bridge. "Did they get a CAT scan?" I ask. "Okay, order a urine culture and a Vitamin B12 and folic acid level. I'll see him when I get on the unit. No, I don't have time to talk with the daughter right now."

I arrive at Medical Records, pick up a stack of charts, and head for the dictation room. A couple of the charts are for 24-hour admissions. I thought the history and physical were sufficient, but now Joint Commission requires dictated history and physical, plus a dictated discharge summary. To me, that seems a waste of my time, having to repeat the exact same information twice. I don't want the hassle of losing my admitting privileges today, so I dictate the redundancy. I dictate for an hour and then head to the Psych Unit for treatment team staffing, where all of the inpatients will have their treatment plans updated.

At the staffing are registered nurses Gwen and Linda, therapist Debbie, social workers Ann Marie and Xavier George, psychologist Leigh Ann, recreational therapist Kay, and a few pharmacy students. The first patient to be discussed has no more days approved and nowhere to return to, so she must be discharged to the shelter. If not, the hospital will have to eat the bill and I won't get paid. She refuses to go to the shelter. Her husband is angry because we aren't allowed to give him information about her, at her request. He threatened to come to the hospital and if not allowed to see her, contact his attorney

"Tell her she has to go tomorrow," I said. "See if the pharmacy can give her a couple of weeks of free medication, since she has no money. Get her a follow-up appointment at the Mental Health Center."

Another patient is still refusing all her medications

because the voices are telling her she doesn't need them. She thinks she will wait for Jesus to heal her. "If Jesus doesn't make it by this evening," I tell them, "we need to give her IM Haldol and Ativan. How many days do we have left for her?" Another patient withdrawing from alcohol is going into DT's. He's taking almost all the time of one of our two health care technicians and the patient coming from the Emergency Room will probably tie up the other technician. Two patients will be discharged tomorrow, so little time is spent discussing their cases. The final patient needs a nursing home, but can't be discharged until a PASAR number is received from Medicaid. In the meantime, Medicare is pressuring for the patient to be discharged. Hospital administration is hinting to not admit so many of these patients because the hospital loses money on these cases. The patient is resisting going to a nursing home and wants to return home to live alone. This is not an option. The children are fighting over who will inherit what, and have missed the last two meetings with the social worker. I tell my team "Keep looking for an intermediate level of care facility. Let's keep our fingers crossed that the number will come in this week."

The meeting is adjourned and will reassemble at the same time next week.

Next stop, Critical Care Unit. The consult patient is a 21 year-old single white female college student who took fifteen of her roommate's sleeping pills after her boyfriend of six months broke up with her. This is her fourth suicide attempt. Last year, she made superficial cuts of both wrists with a plastic knife. She is followed at student health on campus.

"How are you feeling?" I ask her. "Looks like you had a pretty close call. What's going on to make you feel like killing yourself?"

"I don't know," she tells me. "I feel so stupid. Todd came by to see me. Can I go home now?"

I spend about twenty minutes collecting information and assessing her potential of harming herself in the foreseeable future. I then write in her chart that she is cleared psychiatrically and that she needs to see her therapist within forty-eight hours.

CCU Nurses are very helpful because their favorite part of treating so called *psych patients* is the discharge. I dictate a consult note and head for the office.

That turned out to be an easy consult, and I'm glad she didn't require admission to Behavioral Medicine: that would have taken several more minutes of my time. At the office, Pia has several forms requiring my signature and she reminds me to take some Zoloft samples for an indigent patient in Reidsville. The phone rings and it turns out to be the case reviewer from one of the managed care companies. The doctor at the other end of the phone is cordial and soft spoken. I tell him that the patient has not made much progress and that I'd like to keep her in the hospital for three more days. I end up getting one day because she mentioned thinking about suicide, but had no current plan or intent. He tells me I can appeal his decision.

"Forget it, thank you and have a nice day," I tell him. Besides, appeal to whom? And why would someone else approve what he did not? Appealing a case usually is a waste of time. I'm better off using that time to do something I can get paid for. Today, I'm seeing patients in my Reidsville office. It's around a 40-minute drive, if there are no tractors, little old ladies, or school buses on the narrow highway. I'll stop for a burger on the way. This is my thinking time, so I put in my Al Green CD or a Book on Tape, if I've purchased anything interesting lately.

The Reidsville office is always busy, so I pray for appointment no-shows in order to get a break. The mental health center is starting to farm patients out into the communities, since they will no longer be able to offer services. This is due to mental health reform occurring across the nation. There are about four private providers in this whole county, so waits-to-be-seen will become longer and longer. It was overheard that mental health services at the county jail were better. At least the law requires prisoners to be seen in fourteen days.

I'm being a bit sarcastic here, but until someone shows me differently, I see a potential disaster ahead for those in need of mental health care. Simple math, physics, social science, and common sense seem to suggest that something very bad is about to become even worse in our society. I believe a problem is not being fixed, but the buck is being passed. I hope and pray that I am wrong. The big question is: Where will it stop? On our streets, in our jails, in our public facilities, in your home, where? Most are betting on the private sector. If there's money to be made, the private sector will be right to the rescue. I believe that the real problem is lack of funding. Creative ideas, like a state lottery, can't be the way, because it is sinful. More acceptable is cutting the budget of mental health programs and praying that everything will be alright. Allowing people to just do without needed care isn't considered sinful.

There are three patients in the waiting room. I'm thirty minutes late due to the unplanned events at the hospital. I pick up my stack of charts and head toward the interview room, where I sit and try to focus on seeing patients. Leigh, the receptionist, brings the first patient back. "So, how have you been Mrs. J?"

"Not too good. That new medicine didn't agree with me."

"Oh yeah? How long were you able to take it?"

"I took it one time and I started having all those side effects the pharmacist gave me the papers on. Then I heard on TV that it's causing people to commit suicide. My daughter looked it up on the Internet and there were about twenty different side effects. I took the Klonopins though. They work real well; I need some more."

"Don't you remember me talking to you for thirty minutes about how you have to wait a few weeks for the medicine to get in your system? Side effects are usually rare and mild enough that only one in ten patients have to stop taking the medicine."

"Well, I guess I must be that one then."

"Klonopin is a very good medicine for short term and occasional use, but taking it for long periods can lead to dependence. After a while, you will need more and more medicine to get the same effect. That's not what we want, because that will be adding to your problems. By the way, did you keep that appointment with the therapist we made two weeks ago?"

"No, I didn't."

"Why not?"

"I was feeling better on those Klonopins, so I didn't see any reason to."

"Do you remember me talking about how important psychotherapy is, in addition to taking your medications, in order for you to reach a full recovery?"

"No, all I remember is about the Klonopins. I know the blue ones work a lot better than those green ones. Two yellow ones might work just as well, though. Do they come in other colors?"

The insurance company will give me twenty minutes to re-educate, re-evaluate, and try to communicate something meaningful to this patient. Then everything must be correctly documented, and if the wrong billing code is sent in, I won't even get paid. It would be one of those *"we got you that time"* moments. I don't think it's hard to see why a doctor might be tempted to just give the patient that bottle of blue Klonopin and send her on her merry way. Even Ray Charles can see that's all she's interested in. It's likely she has recently visited some other doctor who refused her Klonopin because of her non-compliance with treatment. That doctor was afraid of getting in trouble with the DEA, since Klonopin is a controlled drug. I could refuse her Klonopin and allow her to visit the next unsuspecting doctor, or I could try and compromise by looking for an anti depressant that I may be able to convince her to take *along with* the Klonopin. I could tell her no more Klonopin, unless she gets into therapy and approaches the problem from other angles. But what do I know? I'm just a dumb-ass psychiatrist with only twelve years of training.

Sometimes patients perceive us as dumb, but little do they know that there is nothing they can come up with that we haven't heard many times before. I often do give them the benefit of the doubt, or give them enough rope to hang themselves. Many patients are arrested in that adolescent *know everything they need* stage. For them, I say "First do no harm," because it's going to be a while before any meaningful progress can be made with this type of patient...if ever. Hopefully, that denial will one day weaken, if they live long enough. All you can really do is to confront the behavior and hope that reality sinks in for them one day.

Next patient is brought in by his rest home operator. He is seventy-nine years old and beginning to lose his memory. He can't sleep well at night, sometimes hears voices, and follows up every three or four months for a med check. He is starting to adjust to his new environment; he's calm and smiles appropriately. This is a big change from six months ago, when he had become combative toward staff, was always agitated, and had to be watched like a hawk 24/7. All he needs today is refills for his prescriptions. The visit is quick and uneventful and the patient has stabilized nicely.

"Tell Leigh to schedule his next appointment for four months," I tell him. "And have a nice summer, sir."

Next patient is Little Johnny, who has ADHD and a behavioral problem. The new medicine has helped marginally, but he still gets into a couple of fights weekly and he failed his last math exam. Little Johnny sits on the sofa calmly for as long as he can, but in about five minutes he starts to talk incessantly about all kinds of topics and roams about the room exploring various objects, despite his mothers objections. A few minutes later he is standing on his head ready to do cartwheels.

"Okay Little Johnny, I think I know what you need." I increase his Ritalin and add some Clonidine. His mother is good with instructions so they're finished quickly. "If he's not improving in a week, give me a call."

Anne, the nurse/therapist I work with, comes in between patients, stating that she thinks Mrs. K is manic and needs hospitalization. We review the particulars and the admission is approved. "Have the on call nurse admit them to my service, I'll see her this evening."

Leigh asks if I have time to see a couple of pharmaceutical representatives. I say "Tell them I have about five minutes to talk with them." Pharmaceutical reps are a valuable resource because of the continuing education they provide, along with drug samples. Dinner programs aren't bad either. Two young and vibrant people come in and review the latest drug study of their product. Presentations are succinct and informative. I sign for the samples and they're on their way.

On this particular day, I end up seeing about twelve patients in the clinic. Diagnoses vary from panic disorder, bipolar disorder, psychotic depression, adjustment disorder, polysubstance dependence, chronic pain disorder, and borderline and dependent personality disorders. I finally finish up the paper work and head back to Burlington to begin the work-up on today's three admissions. Depending on the circumstances, I may save certain parts of the exam for the next day, since I have twenty-four hours to complete the full history and physical exam. I complete any left-over rounding at this time, then enter new orders and progress notes into the computer.

Next, I'm on the road headed across town to Residential Treatment Services (R.T.S.). On the way, the cell phone rings. The nurse from the unit needs some orders clarified. She gives me a heads-up that a well-known patient is in the Emergency Room trying to gain admission. I say *"Lay low and see what the ER doc recommends."* I hope I won't have to hear about her again at 3:00 am.

At RTS there are two detox patients, one with a history of delirium tremens, which is a potentially fatal condition in one out of twenty patients. I do his physical exam and make sure he has adequate medications to minimize the risk of withdrawal seizures or other complications. The first 48 hours are the riskiest for the onset of seizures. DT's usually occur around Day Five. The county pays for a three-day stay, due to limited funding. The math somehow doesn't add up, but a few more days' extension is possible, if the proper form is filled out correctly. The other patient's drug of choice is crack cocaine, so he will just experience depression and craving, but no life-threatening concerns. He generally smokes up to $300 worth a day, even without a regular job. I tell him that I would like him to try a medication called Wellbutrin to help ease his cravings. He refuses on the grounds that he doesn't like taking medication, plus he heard that anti-depressants cause people to commit suicide. He may last for three days, if he doesn't succumb to cravings for the drug and take off to get more crack.

Thirty minutes later I'm headed for Raleigh to see some inmates. I may seem to be overworked and sometimes I am, but somehow I've found myself in these places where nobody else cares to be, places where people's needs seem to be ignored by the higher establishment. I know I can't fix the world, but I feel it's up to me to at least make a start and do what I can. My hope is that, at some point, others will join and give back to the communities. Or maybe a politician will do the right thing.

I love this country with all my heart and I've learned to let racial intolerance or ignorance roll off me like water off a duck's back. I don't wait for others to do something, if I feel in my heart that I might be able to make a difference. The next segregation will not be racial, but based on class. The dynamic will be the same, however. I have lived most of my life between the Have Nots and the Haves and I've experienced both first-hand.

It is not a theory or speculation that the gap between the two is widening. It has already started to happen, and if this country doesn't properly care for its citizens, America will continue to die from within. The Taliban or other terrorists won't have to destroy us. In the long run, spending on unnecessary wars that spawn other wars may lead to a karmic payback, as history has always proven. At this time, we are in a position to help more people than at anytime in the history of mankind. A superior military is essential, but we've always had that. The new precedence of pre-emptive strike may have made future wars more likely.

If a cumulative resistance ever does peak, it will probably make Saddam Hussein look like a Boy Scout. We will have blown the opportunity to have adequate health and mental health care for all Americans, adequate employment opportunities, housing, and childcare. The chance to do some real good, such as ending world hunger once and for all, will have been lost. If we can put a man on the moon, there is nothing on earth we can't accomplish—if it's what the people want.

The outcome of the conflict in the Middle East will tell us clearly if the best path is being taken and if the lives and money invested will pay future dividends or be a bust. At this moment in history, only time will tell for sure.

EPILOGUE

I sincerely hope you have enjoyed reading Evolution of a Psychiatrist, Against the Odds as much as I enjoyed writing it. Most physicians decide to enter the field of medicine to help people. If only it were that simple. It's similar to Michael Jordan, when he left Chapel Hill telling the world that he was going into professional basketball so that all the fans and coaches in the world would love him. The reality is, they all respect him because he clearly earned the respect of every sports fan. I doubt that many of the fans and coaches of his opponents really felt a lot of affection and endearment toward him during the playoffs, especially after a fifty-point game-winning performance.

The lesson here is that no matter how great you become, there will always be those who dislike you and for whom you can never do anything beneficial. This is because those individuals are not open to receive what you may have to give them. They have their own construct of the world and you may be considered by them as a means to an end, if that much. That's really the sad part about practicing general psychiatry.

There are days when I encounter individuals who certainly can be helped so simply, by just saying "Doctor I respect your wisdom, knowing that God allowed you to receive it. I trust that you will do your best to help me regain my health, or establish a healthier way of living my life. I plan to have my own ego take a break and rest awhile, since it was its overindulgence that brought me to where I am today. I am willing to look past my walls of denial, if you think I should and, as you said, you will be available to assist me with this challenge. I will gladly pay your fee and I will do my best to follow your instruction."

This is the way psychiatric medicine was intended to be practiced. It was meant to be a solemn contract between patient and doctor. The expectations were clear: If your services weren't desired, there was no problem. The patient made the decision based on free will.

Today, there exist so much interference and unsolicited biased information that the patient has consulted the barber, maintenance man, brother-in-law, TV reporter, website, magazine subscription, and the lady at the checkout counter, before finally think that seeing a mental health professional might be an acceptable idea. To drive the point home, I doubt that someone going on a flight to New York would enter the cockpit and start suggesting to the pilot which route to take, or would be allowed to fly the plane because they had read an article on flying jumbo jets. Just as unlikely, would a person suggest to their auto mechanic the latest technique for increasing engine torque, because a relative who knows a mechanic heard him talking to a race car driver about it? Those two cases are totally absurd, but lo and behold, it's a common thing to assess patients who already know what they need to make their nervous system function like new. They already know that what you prescribe will not work. They may play the game, but their agenda is already decided.

In this particular patient type, the simple truth is that they don't really want to change their lives. They just need something to help shine a spotlight on their misery, because it can be very lonely at times. It's like the door to the cage is wide open, yet they know nothing other than the cage, so they are most content staying in the cage and complaining about being in the cage, instead of exploring the freedom outside the cage.

Fear becomes a familiar partner to the point that any behavior that may diminish the fear, such as getting familiar with the outside of the cage, is greatly resisted unconsciously. Without the fear, the complaining must cease, and the complaining has become their main means of communicating with the exterior world.

Misery is the most loyal of friends. "My back is killing me" means I need some affection. "My head aches" means give me your attention. "Medications don't work for me" means there's no love in my life. "I cannot sleep" means comfort me.

The vocabulary is endless. For me, there is nothing more frustrating than to look back over everything I went through over years and years, to finally get to this person and help to free them from their bondage, only to find out that they unconsciously prefer being in bondage. This gives them the best of both worlds: they can blame me for them not getting any better, yet they can still enjoy their misery.

In parting, I wish to leave a message for all misery lovers.

Please, *don't* come to see me.

Kenneth Jay Headen, MD Psychiatrist

Made in the USA